Dublin Tales

Dublin
Tales

Stories selected and edited by
Paul Delaney and
Eve Patten

Series editor
Helen Constantine

OXFORD
UNIVERSITY PRESS

OXFORD
UNIVERSITY PRESS

Great Clarendon Street, Oxford, OX2 6DP,
United Kingdom

Oxford University Press is a department of the University of Oxford.
It furthers the University's objective of excellence in research, scholarship,
and education by publishing worldwide. Oxford is a registered trade mark of
Oxford University Press in the UK and in certain other countries

Published in the United States of America by Oxford University Press
198 Madison Avenue, New York, NY 10016, United States of America

British Library Cataloguing in Publication Data

Data available

Library of Congress Control Number: 2023940971

ISBN 9780192855558

DOI: 10.1093/oso/9780192855558.001.0001

Printed and bound by
CPI Group (UK) Ltd, Croydon, CR0 4YY

MIX
Paper | Supporting
responsible forestry
FSC
www.fsc.org
FSC® C013604

Contents

Picture Credits

Introduction

'Tell me this', an exasperated Dubliner asks the indo-lent student-narrator of Flann O'Brien's *At Swim-Two-Birds* (1939), 'do you ever open a book at all?' In an age where pessimists often bemoan falling levels of reading, the collapse of the publishing industry, and the death of print, Dublin is a place where books continue to be pro-duced and read. It is a city with an illustrious literary heritage, where writers are rightly celebrated and where stories are etched into the streetscape. Statues of some of Dublin's most famous authors have become landmarks: Oscar Wilde in Merrion Square; James Joyce on North Earl Street; Brendan Behan on the Royal Canal; George Bernard Shaw inside the National Gallery. Public spaces feature busts of acclaimed poets, plaques outside build-ings tell of once distinguished inhabitants, and gable ends are decorated with portraits of cherished authors. Some writers have become synonymous with historic locations (W. B. Yeats, Lady Gregory, and the Abbey Theatre, for instance, or Jonathan Swift and St Patrick's Cathedral, or Patrick Kavanagh and the Grand Canal); others have had their names attached to recent architectural projects (Joyce, Samuel Beckett, and Sean O'Casey each have bridges on the River Liffey named for them); others still have given voice to parts of the city often omitted from travel guides and history books (novelist Roddy Doyle and poet Paula Meehan are two contemporary champions of the disenfranchised). Belatedly, in March 2021, Mary Lavin was remembered in a street name, becoming the first Irish woman writer to be bestowed such an honour in the capital city.

If literature is central to the way Dublin represents itself to itself, it is also vital to the city's tourist industry, with Fáilte Ireland (Ireland's tourist board) making much of the capital's artistic life, and businesses and souvenir shops trading in the commodification of its heritage. Several pubs continue to profit from their associations with the city's literary past (McDaids, Davy Byrnes, Mulligan's, the Palace Bar), while tour companies bring devotees to some of Dublin's feted locales (Bram Stoker's birthplace in Fairview, Joyce's Martello Tower in Sandycove, Patrick Pearse's school, St Enda's, in Rathfarnham). Fittingly, excerpts from the city's most renowned book, *Ulysses* (1922), are inscribed into Dublin's pathways, with a weathered series of beautiful brass plates set into the pavement of the city centre, commemorating the protagonist

Leopold Bloom's fictional journey across his hometown on the 16 June 1904—the day that is now Dublin's annual Bloomsday festival.

In recognition of Dublin's rich literary heritage, the city was awarded UNESCO City of Literature status in 2010, becoming only the fourth international city to be so honoured. This award was granted in acknowledgement of Dublin's contribution to world literature; it was also presented because of the city's commitment to lived literary practice. Love of the written word is very much part of the life of the city, which is home to a constellation of libraries, bookshops, periodicals, and publishing houses. Tramp Press, New Island Books, Liberties Press, Arlen House, Dedalus Press, and Skein Press are just some of the exciting independent publishers based in Dublin, while *The Stinging Fly*, *The Dublin Review*, *Poetry Ireland Review*, *Cyphers*, and *Comhar* are amongst the city's most brilliant magazines and literary journals. Dublin is also the setting for numerous reading groups and writing circles; it hosts an array of festivals and exhibitions; and it contains several major universities, where literature is taught, supported, promoted, and researched (including Trinity College Dublin, University College Dublin, and Dublin City University). The National Library, the Dublin Writers' Museum, the Irish Writers' Centre, Marsh's Library, and the Museum of Literature Ireland (MoLI) are just some of the institutions that help to preserve the city's literary heritage, while the Gate, the Abbey, the Gaiety, and Smock Alley are a few of the capital's most historic and energetic theatre venues. The city council sponsors the prestigious International Dublin Literary Award, drawing nominations from libraries, and from library users, throughout the world. Dublin City Council and Dublin City Libraries also host the annual One Dublin One Book initiative, which encourages everyone in the city to read a designated book connected with the capital during the month of April each year.

Dublin Tales exemplifies the Irish capital city's commitment to literary practice. This volume comprises seventeen short stories by writers from across the last 120 years. It includes authors who are, or were, native Dubliners; authors from other parts of the country who live, or have lived, in the city; and authors from overseas who have made Dublin their home. A few of the writers included in the collection are international names (one is arguably the most influential English-language novelist of the twentieth century); others may be less familiar to readers. Some of the tales have been anthologized many times before, others are collected here for the first time, and four of the stories were commissioned specially for this volume. The book also includes bilingual versions of two stories that were originally written in the Irish language—Dara

Ó Conaola's 'I nGleic' and Caitlín Nic Íomhair's 'Cíocras', which are translated by the authors, respectively, as 'In a Pickle' and 'Relentless'. Irish remains one of the two official languages of Ireland, and has immense historical, cultural, and literary significance; it is a living language for a sizeable proportion of the Irish population, and it is the medium through which a number of contemporary authors express themselves. For these reasons, the stories by Ó Conaola and Nic Íomhair are included in both Irish and English. Overall, the stories in *Dublin Tales* are variously humorous and haunting, intimate and violent, mundane and bizarre. Read as a collection, they illustrate the diverse and often innovative ways in which short fiction has been practised in Ireland.

'Isn't the implicit promise of an anthology that it will, or aspires to, present something different, unexpected', Joyce Carol Oates wrote thirty years ago, in her introduction to *The Oxford Book of American Short Stories* (1992). 'Do editors of anthologies consult only other anthologies, instead of reading original collections of stories?' The imperative to look past the example of previous editors is fundamental to any act of anthologization. So is the need to read beyond original collections of stories, to consider work that only appeared in magazines, that was broadcast on the radio, or that has been produced in digital format. Equally, it is to be expected that anthologizers should seek out fresh stories, resisting the temptation to turn to the predictable or the pre-packaged. As Sinéad Gleeson remarked in her collection of Irish short fiction, *The Art of the Glimpse* (2020), the anthology is a generous art form since it constitutes 'a gift' or 'a gathering of possibilities' for the unsuspecting reader. Within its pages, established and emerging writers can be placed in generative company, forgotten works can be recalled, contemporary stories can be showcased, lesser-known tales can be given prominence, and celebrated texts can be re-energized as they are placed in new or surprising contexts. That is the promise of such books, and it is something we have tried to realize in *Dublin Tales*. Inevitably, this has meant that some authors have had to step aside to allow space for other writers to be represented. Roddy Doyle, Anne Enright, Maeve Brennan, Christine Dwyer Hickey, Dermot Bolger, Maeve Binchy, Sally Rooney, Nuala O'Connor, and Kevin Barry are just some of the illustrious, well-anthologized figures to give way in this instance.

Not only do the stories in *Dublin Tales* encompass work by a range of famous and less familiar authors, covering a variety of forms and aesthetic styles, they also offer glimpses into the recent history of the city. Many of the stories depict Dubliners engaged in the most ordinary of activities: travelling on a bus in Éilís Ní Dhuibhne's 'Miss Moffat Goes to Town'; placating a screaming infant in Caitriona Lally's 'Tramlines'; or negotiating unwanted gifts from an elderly relative in Brendan Behan's 'The Confirmation Suit'. Some stories speak to older times, mentioning parts of the city that have long since been redeveloped or renamed. James Stephens' 'A Rhinoceros, Some Ladies, and a Horse' includes reference to Dan Lowrey's Theatre, for instance, an elegant music hall on Dublin's Dame Street, which became the Olympia Theatre in the 1920s; this much-loved venue was recently renamed the 3Olympia in an act of corporate branding that some have likened to cultural vandalism. Other stories map a city whose streetscape has barely changed over the last hundred years. The path Lenehan traverses in James Joyce's 'Two Gallants' can easily be retraced by a contemporary visitor to the city, for example, while brave (or foolhardy) sightseers can test the urban legend that Mary O'Donnell records in 'The Black Church'—if you walk three times, anti-clockwise, around St Mary's Chapel of Ease (the Black Church), at midnight, you will see the Devil.

Many of the stories in *Dublin Tales* describe the city at peace. Some, however, capture it at moments of unrest, testifying to the fact that Dublin has also been a setting for insurrections, terrorist attacks, and other crises over the course of its extended history. In 'The Black Church', a child of the inner-city tenements struggles to make sense of the 1916 Easter Rising; in 'The Sniper', the awfulness of internecine conflict is sketched by Liam O'Flaherty in an archetypal story of the Irish Civil War (1922–23); and in Val Mulkerns' 'Four Green Fields', the atrocity of a loyalist bombing on Talbot Street in 1974 (and, by implication, the horrors of the thirty-year period called 'the Troubles') is captured with indignation and disbelief. Elizabeth Bowen's 'Unwelcome Idea' takes the tramline south to Dún Laoghaire, and sketches fragments of a conversation between passengers about air raid precautions during World War Two (euphemistically known as 'the Emergency' by the Irish government of the time). John McGahern's 'Sierra Leone' is also set against a backdrop of international anxiety, as an illicit affair unfolds in the early 1960s, contemporaneous with the Cuban Missile Crisis and the early stages of decolonization in west Africa.

Bowen's and McGahern's stories serve as a timely reminder that Dublin has never been a mere parochial city, and that influences and ideas have always come from without, often enriching—but sometimes destabilizing—traditional mores and inherited practices. In some of the more recent stories in *Dublin Tales* these influences are intensified, as writers engage with the impact, as well as with the experience, of immigration, multiculturalism, and social media in a contemporary context. Melatu Uche

Okorie's 'Arrival' follows a Nigerian woman travelling south, from Belfast airport to Swords in North County Dublin, to meet her future husband for the first time; Ní Dhuibhne's 'Miss Moffat Goes to Town' captures something of the multilingual energy of the inner city; and Mirsad Ibišević's debut story, 'The Emigrant', depicts a young Bosnian refugee struggling to adapt to Irish life, traumatized by the murder of his family in former Yugoslavia in the early 1990s. Such stories stress the city's links to the larger world, reminding readers that Dublin is as much a global city as it is Ireland's capital.

Dublin is a 'city of talk, gossip, rumour, scandal', the late poet Brendan Kennelly enthused in *Dublines* (1996). It is a city with a passion for stories, where the versatility of conversation is highly valued, and where boldness of discourse is often deemed praiseworthy. A number of stories in *Dublin Tales* speak to this, not least 'The Confirmation Suit', with its vibrant narrative mode, 'A Rhinoceros, Some Ladies, and a Horse', which is almost acrobatic in its verbal dexterity, and 'Miss Moffat Goes to Town', which opens with the most impossible of threats being directed at the justifiably puzzled Miss Moffat. Other stories are more hesitant in their negotiation of what can—or, indeed, what should—be said in certain situations, mindful of the extent to which reticence and reserve have also been encouraged in the city's communities.

Dublin Tales is arranged chronologically, reflecting the time in which the authors lived and the contexts in which the stories were produced. The stories don't have to be read consecutively, as each text is discrete and stands on its own. Indeed, one of the most rewarding aspects of compiling this anthology has been discovering different ways that the stories interact with and speak to one another across time. In some instances, these links are self-evident: the title of William Trevor's 'Two More Gallants' identifies Joyce's 'Two Gallants' as an obvious antecedent. It is a suggestive choice since the latter text especially pleased the older writer. 'It is one of the most important stories in the book' that would become *Dubliners* (1914), Joyce famously wrote in the summer of 1906, as he struggled to get his collection published amidst concerns of vulgarity, obscenity, and potential libel. 'I would rather sacrifice five of the other stories (which I could name) than this one.' Echoes of 'Two Gallants', and of Joyce more generally, can be detected in other contemporary stories, most notably in Kevin Power's 'Catastrophe', which weaves a poignant tale of writerly vulnerability into a mischievous satire of Dublin's literati.

Additional connections can be drawn between the stories in *Dublin Tales*, with themes such as historical legacy, the consequences of violence, social inequality, sexual desire, the primacy of the imagination, and acts of travel recurring throughout the collection. Several stories also depict the varied ways that Dubliners think about their 'glorified kip of a city', in the memorable words of Rashers Tierney, one of the characters in James Plunkett's panoramic novel of the capital, *Strumpet City* (1969). A point of particular interest is the uses to which the classic stereotype of the Irish mother is put by different writers in *Dublin Tales*, and the boldness of George Egerton's early twentieth-century tale, 'Mammy', in this respect. In Egerton's story, the eponymous Mammy is neither a mother, nor an image of Mother Ireland, nor a cipher for the Virgin Mary; instead, she is a brothel keeper who fights to secure the last rites for a young woman dying of tuberculosis in a deeply judgemental Catholic society.

The setting of 'Mammy' is the storied (but now vanished) area of Monto, a huge red-light district that once comprised a significant part of the north inner city, later reimagined as 'Nighttown' in *Ulysses*, and the subject of a few bawdy songs by the legendary folk band The Dubliners. It is one of several instances in *Dublin Tales* where stories demonstrate how reciprocal the relationship can be between place and literary practice. Just as Dublin is embedded in the literary imagination, so literature, in turn, has helped to give definition to aspects of the city's life and to its sense of spatial history. Specific sites are identified throughout the collection that are crucial to the design of particular tales. The imposing statue of the nineteenth-century parliamentarian, Daniel O'Connell, on O'Connell Street, for instance, is central to Dara Ó Conaola's story 'I nGleic' ('In a Pickle'), and sparks an audaciously surreal narrative of rebellion and constraint. Grafton Street, the GPO, Trinity College, St Stephen's Green, the Phoenix Park, and the Docklands are just some of the other locations that are described with affection by writers in *Dublin Tales*.

Long-standing rivalries between Dublin's northside and southside are represented at different points in the volume, underscoring the symbolic importance of the River Liffey, which dissects the heart of the city. 'Miss Moffat Goes to Town' and 'Tramlines' offer exemplary instances of this. In the first of these two stories, Ní Dhuibhne's narrator wryly remarks of Miss Moffat's relocation from the southside to the northside of the city that 'it is a journey which very few people make in their lives. Migration is generally in the opposite direction. On good days she feels brave, and on bad days, foolhardy'. In Lally's story, by contrast, the anonymous protagonist is said to cringe at the sight of 'people from the other side of the river day-tripping' on the northside once the Luas tramline was extended across the Liffey: 'they couldn't hide their astonishment that there was a world beyond Ranelagh or Dundrum, that some parts of the northside are *actually ok*'. In a few of the earlier tales, the city is depicted as an incestuous space that is easily negotiated, where everyone knows—or at least knows about—one another. (Joyce offers a classic example of this.) In some of the more recent texts, by contrast, Dublin seems an increasingly imprecise locale, where people have become anonymized, and where the city's soul appears to be threatened by the forces of globalization, multinational investment, estate sprawl, and the growth of the commuter belt. In Caitlín Nic Íomhair's 'Cíocras' ('Relentless') this is given an added inflection, when a young woman finds herself cut off from the rest of the city—trapped with her married lover, in the increasingly claustrophobic space of her apartment—because of the Covid pandemic and the awkward announcement of a national lockdown.

The variety and multiplicity of the city that is Dublin is reflected in the words of Katie, the protagonist of Lia Mills's delicate novel *Fallen* (2014), which was the One Dublin One Book choice a few years ago: 'I had walked through the world blinkered, blind to its texture and deaf to its music; now I discovered cities within the city.' The stories assembled in *Dublin Tales* allow readers to discover for themselves cities within the city, and to encounter the many versions of Dublin that speak to us, across time and space, through the resonant storytelling of some of Ireland's finest prose writers.

Paul Delaney and Eve Patten,
Trinity College Dublin.

Mammy

George Egerton
(Mary Chavelita
Dunne Bright)

One soft October night, in the year when *la belle France* wept for the loss of her fair provinces to the victorious Prussian, theatre-goers in Dublin city—a gay, responsive crowd—thronging out after the play, were met by the rattle of fire-engines, the imperative clangour of bells, and the raucous cries of the drivers as they urged their horses into a gallop.

The windows and the roofs were crowded with spectators. A lurid background of sky, alternately brightened by darting spears of golden flame, or dulled by curling rifts of murky smoke, could be seen through a break in some tall houses—a big whiskey distillery was burning riotously.

Obeying the peculiar communicative shudder that seems to hypnotize a crowd and suggest a solidarity of action on the part of each unit, however dissimilar, strings of outside cars, driven by excited jarvies and carrying men in evening dress and women in theatre wraps, were dashing towards the scene of the fire to the accompanying foot-beats of an eager, curious crowd.

Near the fire itself the streets were densely packed with people, hindering the working of the hose and the change of suburban engines to the rescue, while patrols of mounted police backed their admirably trained horses against the breast of the crowd to keep the roadway clear. The sky, the air, the people, the very inanimate buildings seemed to palpitate with a common movement. The spire of a tall red church glowed like a brazen pillar, and the profuse gilding and fretted scroll-work on every pinnacle seemed painted in flame, the statues of the saints glowing effulgently.

The night resounded with the unforgettable shriek of horses in terror, the despairing bay of a hound imprisoned in the distillery yard, the hoarse cries of men, the hissing rush of the water torrents, the hollow booming roar of flame, and the crash of falling beams. And behind and beyond all, the peculiar hush of night, almost a distinct sound by contrast of its very quiet, reigned supreme—making all other sounds, even the breathing of the crowd that was an unconscious sobbing indrawal as of one breath, seem sounds in the foreground. The dense mass of people, staring with upturned, crimson faces, glistening eyes, and gaping mouths, merely added a human note to the conflagration.

As the casks of raw spirit were broached it ran along the street and gutters, a dancing river of fretful blue flame, making the crowd jump like Dervishes, and the horses rear as it touched their feet.

The 'Liberty' was threatened; its narrow, noisome alleys made clearance dangerously difficult; the dwellers in the grand old mansions, rich in oak panelling, carved mantelboard, and superb staircases, long since degraded into filthy tenements, were hurling their frowsy bedding and dilapidated chattels on to the heads of the frenzied crowd below—frenzied, for they had broken into the crockery shops, and, seizing every available utensil, regardless of its destined use, dipped it into the flaming stream, and gulped it down as it cooled; some had taken off a boot and hopped on one leg as they drank from this unsavoury beaker.

Once an awed hush stole over the crowd, and it pressed back to make a passage for a weird procession. Three hags keened shrilly as they preceded six half-sobered men, bearing a wretched pallet bed, upon which lay the corpse of a man, with his chin tied up. The flames played in lambent phosphorescence over the tallow, mask-like face, waggling and sliding as the bearers swayed under the weight; one stiff, white, cotton-socked foot stuck out with a derisive effect. It passed; once more the crowd drank recklessly, and burst into ribald oaths and canting songs; and the stress of the surging waters, and booming roar in the heart of the fire, the 'Lick, lick!' of vagabond flamelets, ever searching with curling tongues, filled the air—and the spirit ran, a sparkling river, to the Liffey, and danced in red-gold laminæ on the top of the water like a fiery serpent coiling seaward, to the croon of barges rocking at its side.

A group of outside cars, with a noisy freight of men and women, was drawn up outside a public-house; the street echoed to their laughter, the pop of flying corks, and the growl of the crowd, scrambling for the largesse of silver they had scattered amongst it.

In London (probably not now in Dublin), the brazen advertisement and audacious effrontery of the hetairai, at the time of this incident, in the capital of the most moral country in the world, would challenge belief. Dublin, at all times the most narrow of provincial towns, with a foreign garrison note, rang with their doings. Satin gowns of orange, scarlet, or azure, worn with daring hats at four in the afternoon in Grafton Street, were usual.

When aureate-haired Annie Fitzallen won the Cardinal's celebrated piebald ponies at the Rotunda bazaar, it was said his Eminence unwisely tried to buy them back; and male Dublin, and wives 'in the know', were convulsed at the wording of a note in refusal from 'Nanny' to the Prince of the Church. Respectable Dublin felt set at naught when she drove them with startling harness, jingling bells, and diminutive tiger in attendance; herself attired in a driving coat of cardinal satin, with a knot of ribbon to match on her whip. Yet each morning saw the pavements of the notorious Mecklenburg Street (since changed to Tyrone Street) lined two deep with beggars waiting for food, raiment, or medicine; they never went away empty-handed.

On the night of the great fire this wanton street was comparatively quiet, but the light streamed in fan-like rays from the long line of windows that were all links in one chain, the red glow of the hall lamps echoing the note in the sky above.

Up in an attic room, into which rich bedding and many dainty accessories had been caried with lavish generosity, a girl tossed and sobbed in a semi-delirious stage.

'"*Holy Mary, Mother of God, pray for us sinners, now and at the hours of our death, amen!*" Oh, my God, how can I die at all without seeing a priest?'

A fit of coughing choked the despairing accents and stained her lips; the sweat had plastered the flaxen rings of hair clammily to her brow; the wild, luminous blue eyes glared with a frenzied appeal; and terror and coming death vied with each other in blanching her pinched features, accentuating the hectic stain on the sharp cheek-bones.

An old woman, 'Biddy the Bawd' by name—years ago the loveliest girl on the town, now a hanger-on in the very house to which she was once the most fatal lure—got up from a stool at the fire and covered the girl's wasted limbs, saying soothingly:

'Be quiet, girleen; she sent for the priest. Sure you'll wear yourself out before he comes—and the divil a damn he'll come, either,' she muttered in an aside, pouring some whiskey into a 'dandy' glass.

The door opened, Mrs Sylvester, 'Mammy' to every man in Dublin by sight or acquaintance, entered—big, modelled on grand lines, though over stout; black-browed, with the defiance of some strange pride folded away in her face, with its stern mouth and kindly smile. Her diamonds sparkled and danced, and her satin bodice creaked as she bent over the bed.

'How is she, Biddy?'

'Bad, she won't last the night—she's calling for the priest'—with a sneering blasphemy.

The girl, roused at her voice, stared fixedly, then flung aside the clothes and sprang to the window—a glowing square in the wall. Her eyes closed with terror and she cowered down on her knees, crying in hoarse whispers:

'It's hell, and it will work into your marrow; salt your bones, eat your vitals, gnaw like a red worm that knows no quiet into your very heart. Oh, Mother of God, don't desert me now in my need! I'll burn in it ... I'll burn ... Oh, fetch a priest!' With a frenzied shriek she seized the woman by the sleeve, muttering appeals and looking fearsomely over her shoulder at the burning square.

'Has anyone gone, Biddy?'

The hag roused from her dozing sleep with a stifled oath.

'I sent Joe. He wouldn't go at first, he says they won't come. That there's an order against it since that affair when the Protestants brought up a scandal against poor Father Dempsey, for the hoax was played on him in this very street.'

Mammy put the girl back in bed with soothing touches of her big, well-cared-for white hands with many rings flashing on the capable fingers.

The shadows wavered like smoke up the whitewashed wall, and the girl lay back, her lips moving:

'Little pigs lying in clean straw. Such little, pink pigs. Five dear, little pigs. Oh, Jacky look, do look.'

The tears trickled down her cheeks and she broke into laugher. The woman watched her broodingly. The girl had no claim upon her; she had come there, as scores of others—pretty, delicate, madly reckless. Six weeks ago she had gone to bed with galloping consumption. Mammy had put her up out of the way, and given her the best that money could buy. A medical knowledge of cause and effect did not prevent Mrs Sylvester from numbering clever members of the faculty amongst her friends; the girl had the benefit of their skill.

A knock at the door roused Mammy from her thoughts. A groom came in.

'I went to the vestry, mam; I saw one of the fathers, and he can't come—it's agin a new ordher. The Cardinal's away, and none of the fathers can come without a speshul permit.'

'Did you say,' in a whisper, 'the girl could not live till morning?'

'I did so, mam. He was sorry enough, but he can't come by reason of the ordher.'

The girl was sitting up again. She caught the words and uttered a heartrending cry that checked the laughter downstairs, sobering half-drunken men, and making the women shiver. Her eyes stared hopelessly and sanely at the older woman.

'Hush,' said the latter, 'hush! You shall see the priest. Go for a cab, Joe.'

'There's no use, mam; there's ne'er a wan this side o' the fire; they're all gone to it, every wan.'

Mammy's eyes flashed and narrowed, her lips tightened resolutely. She loosened the girl's grip of her wrist and slipped her to her feet—she was a slip of a thing, five feet at most, wasted to a shadow.

'Kick that old beast at the fire, Joe; then you can go.' The man roused the hag.

'Hand me that dressing-gown, Biddy, and draw on her stockings.' She put the girl's arms through the sleeves of the gown, and seizing the red silk counterpane, wrapped it crosswise about the frail body; then she put her left arm round the thin shoulders and her right arm under the girl's thighs, bidding her, 'Clasp your arms about my neck'; and to Biddy, 'Take the corners of the quilt and tie them under my arm at the waist. It will help.'

She lifted her burden and went from the room down the stairs. In the hall below a man and a girl in a theatre bonnet stood aside in silent amazement, hushing a jest on their lips as they saw her come down with her silk-wrapped fardel, for Mammy's face courted no comment and repelled all offer of help.

She stepped out into the clear, warm night, hatless, crowned with the glory of her dusky hair, her diamonds flashing, her silken shirt sweeping the wet pavement. The girl in her arms muttered prayers and sobbed hysterically in silly relief. The man in the hall slipped some gold into his companion's hand, and, stepping out into the street again, doffed his hat, and stood looking after her with bared head.

Mammy breathed heavily and the veins in her forehead swelled, one vein making a 'v' as it rose; her neck flushed into purple patches at the nape, where the girl's hands were clasped convulsively—it burned as if held by an iron band; and her stays gripped her heart to bursting point, as the ugly cathedral pile loomed ahead of her.

A second time she halted at the enclosing railings, and gasped hoarsely; the sweat broke through the powder on her face, but no merciful Veronica met her on her way. Two men stood aside to let her pass, and a mounted constabulary man reined his horse and sat watching her as a sentinel.

The girl whimpered. On once more; the very pavement seemed to rise in mockery and hit her in the face; she ceased to feel her feet or hear aught save the agonizing throb and quiver through her own frame.

She reached the vestry door, leant with the girl against the wall, and pulled the night-call sharply; the tinkle of the bell echoed flippantly above the sobs of the girl and the woman's gasping efforts for breath.

The door was opened by the young priest who had been called up before, and who had crept to the altar steps to pray for the poor soul to which he had been temporarily forbidden to minister.

He drew back in astonishment. Mammy entered and bade him undo the knot that had strained to tightness;

then she passed through the sacristy door into the incense-laden gloom, and laid her burden on the carpet at the foot of the little side altar, sacred to the Virgin—then bent and roused the girl with tender touch. The heavy eyes opened—and, as they saw the feet of the Christ on the mission cross, mutilated by stress of penitent kissing; the tender outstretched palms of the Virgin maid with the blue stoles dropping over her white robe, and the glow of the wick in the sacred oil of the silver sanctuary lamps, ever burning in token of the chaliced host in the tabernacle, a smile of ineffable content gathered in them and she folded her hands peacefully.

Mammy drew herself up and asked, as she entered the vestry, with a smile that was a strange blending of sadness, cynicism, and pride:

'Do you know me?'

The boyish priest flushed deeply, but looked in her face with quiet eyes.

'A-a-h! By God, if Christ would not come to the sinner, I am a strange one to bring the sinner to Christ! Well, I've done my part, now you do yours. That will bury her.' She had taken a roll of one-pound notes out of her pocket as she spoke and laid them on the table. Something bright flashed from her lashes as she turned to the outer door—and the servant of God held it respectfully open for the daughter of the Magdalen to pass.

Once more she went out into the night, the night that was black in the depths, with the firmament above it radiant as a crown of fire. And may be, even as it happened once before in Bethany, it will take the Christ to balance accounts with Mammy.

Two Gallants

James Joyce

The grey warm evening of August had descended upon the city and a mild warm air, a memory of summer, circulated in the streets. The streets, shuttered for the repose of Sunday, swarmed with a gaily coloured crowd. Like illumined pearls the lamps shone from the summits of their tall poles upon the living texture below which, changing shape and hue unceasingly, sent up into the warm grey evening air an unchanging unceasing murmur.

Two young men came down the hill of Rutland Square. One of them was just bringing a long monologue to a close. The other, who walked on the verge of the path and was at times obliged to step on to the road, owing to his companion's rudeness, wore an amused listening face. He

was squat and ruddy. A yachting cap was shoved far back
from his forehead and the narrative to which he listened
made constant waves of expression break forth over his
face from the corners of his nose and eyes and mouth.
Little jets of wheezing laughter followed one another out
of his convulsed body. His eyes, twinkling with cunning
enjoyment, glanced at every moment towards his companion's face. Once or twice he rearranged the light waterproof which he had slung over one shoulder in toreador
fashion. His breeches, his white rubber shoes and his jauntily slung waterproof expressed youth. But his figure fell
into rotundity at the waist, his hair was scant and grey and
his face, when the waves of expression had passed over it,
had a ravaged look.

When he was quite sure that the narrative had ended he
laughed noiselessly for fully half a minute. Then he said:

—Well! ... That takes the biscuit!

His voice seemed winnowed of vigour; and to enforce
his words he added with humour:

—That takes the solitary, unique and, if I may so call it,
recherché biscuit!

He became serious and silent when he had said this.
His tongue was tired for he had been talking all the afternoon in a public-house in Dorset Street. Most people
considered Lenehan a leech but, in spite of this reputation,

his adroitness and eloquence had always prevented his friends from forming any general policy against him. He had a brave manner of coming up to a party of them in a bar and of holding himself nimbly at the borders of the company until he was included in a round. He was a sporting vagrant armed with a vast stock of stories, limericks and riddles. He was insensitive to all kinds of discourtesy. No one knew how he achieved the stern task of living, but his name was vaguely associated with racing tissues.

—And where did you pick her up, Corley? he asked.

Corley ran his tongue swiftly along his upper lip.

—One night, man, he said, I was going along Dame Street and I spotted a fine tart under Waterhouse's clock and said good-night, you know. So we went for a walk round by the canal and she told me she was a slavey in a house in Baggot Street. I put my arm round her and squeezed her a bit that night. Then next Sunday, man, I met her by appointment. We went out to Donnybrook and I brought her into a field there. She told me she used to go with a dairyman. ... It was fine, man. Cigarettes every night she'd bring me and paying the tram out and back. And one night she brought me two bloody fine cigars— O, the real cheese, you know, that the old fellow used to smoke. ... I was afraid, man, she'd get in the family way. But she's up to the dodge.

—Maybe she thinks you'll marry her, said Lenehan.

—I told her I was out of a job, said Corley. I told her I was in Pim's. She doesn't know my name. I was too hairy to tell her that. But she thinks I'm a bit of class, you know.

Lenehan laughed again, noiselessly.

—Of all the good ones ever I heard, he said, that emphatically takes the biscuit.

Corley's stride acknowledged the compliment. The swing of his burly body made his friend execute a few light skips from the path to the roadway and back again. Corley was the son of an inspector of police and he had inherited his father's frame and gait. He walked with his hands by his sides, holding himself erect and swaying his head from side to side. His head was large, globular and oily; it sweated in all weathers; and his large round hat, set upon it sideways, looked like a bulb which had grown out of another. He always stared straight before him as if he were on parade and, when he wished to gaze after someone in the street, it was necessary for him to move his body from the hips. At present he was about town. Whenever any job was vacant a friend was always ready to give him the hard word. He was often to be seen walking with policemen in plain clothes, talking earnestly. He knew the inner side of all affairs and was fond of delivering final judgements. He spoke without listening to the speech of his companions. His conversation was mainly about himself: what he had said to such a person and what such a person had said to him and what he had said to settle the matter. When he reported these dialogues he aspirated the first letter of his name after the manner of Florentines.

Lenehan offered his friend a cigarette. As the two young men walked on through the crowd Corley occasionally turned to smile at some of the passing girls but Lenehan's gaze was fixed on the large faint moon circled with a double halo. He watched earnestly the passing of the grey web of twilight across its face. At length he said:

—Well … tell me, Corley, I suppose you'll be able to pull it off all right, eh?

Corley closed one eye expressively as an answer.

—Is she game for that? asked Lenehan dubiously. You can never know women.

—She's all right, said Corley. I know the way to get around her, man. She's a bit gone on me.

—You're what I call a gay Lothario, said Lenehan. And the proper kind of Lothario, too!

A shade of mockery relieved the servility of his manner. To save himself he had the habit of leaving his flattery open to the interpretation of raillery. But Corley had not a subtle mind.

—There's nothing to touch a good slavey, he affirmed. Take my tip for it.

—By one who has tried them all, said Lenehan.

—First I used to go with girls, you know, said Corley, unbosoming; girls off the South Circular. I used to take them out, man, on the tram somewhere and pay the tram or take them to a band or a play at the theatre or buy them chocolate and sweets or something that way. I used to spend money on them right enough, he added, in a convincing tone, as if he were conscious of being disbelieved.

But Lenehan could well believe it; he nodded gravely.

—I know that game, he said, and it's a mug's game.

—And damn the thing I ever got out of it, said Corley.

—Ditto here, said Lenehan.

—Only off of one of them, said Corley.

He moistened his upper lip by running his tongue along it. The recollection brightened his eyes. He too gazed at the pale disc of the moon, now nearly veiled, and seemed to meditate.

—She was ... a bit of all right, he said regretfully.

He was silent again. Then he added:

—She's on the turf now. I saw her driving down Earl Street one night with two fellows with her on a car.

—I suppose that's your doing, said Lenehan.

—There was others at her before me, said Corley philosophically.

This time Lenehan was inclined to disbelieve. He shook his head to and fro and smiled.

—You know you can't kid me, Corley, he said.

—Honest to God! said Corley. Didn't she tell me herself?

Lenehan made a tragic gesture.

—Base betrayer! he said.

As they passed along the railings of Trinity College, Lenehan skipped out into the road and peered up at the clock.

—Twenty after, he said.

—Time enough, said Corley. She'll be there all right. I always let her wait a bit.

Lenehan laughed quietly.

—Ecod! Corley, you know how to take them, he said.

—I'm up to all their little tricks, Corley confessed.

—But tell me, said Lenehan again, are you sure you can bring this off all right? You know it's a ticklish job. They're damn close on that point. Eh? ... What?

His bright, small eyes searched his companion's face for reassurance. Corley swung his head to and fro as if to toss aside an insistent insect, and his brows gathered.

—I'll pull it off, he said. Leave it to me, can't you?

Lenehan said no more. He did not wish to ruffle his friend's temper, to be sent to the devil and told that his advice was not wanted. A little tact was necessary. But Corley's brow was soon smooth again. His thoughts were running another way.

—She's a fine decent tart, he said, with appreciation; that's what she is.

They walked along Nassau Street and then turned into Kildare Street. Not far from the porch of the club a harpist stood in the roadway, playing to a little ring of listeners. He plucked at the wires heedlessly, glancing quickly from time to time at the face of each new-comer and from time to time, wearily also, at the sky. His harp too, heedless that her coverings had fallen about her knees, seemed weary alike of the eyes of strangers and of her master's hands. One hand played in the bass the melody of *Silent, O Moyle*, while the other hand careered in the treble after each group of notes. The notes of the air throbbed deep and full.

The two young men walked up the street without speaking, the mournful music following them. When they reached Stephen's Green they crossed the road. Here the noise of trams, the lights and the crowd released them from their silence.

—There she is! said Corley.

At the corner of Hume Street a young woman was standing. She wore a blue dress and a white sailor hat. She stood on the curbstone, swinging a sunshade in one hand. Lenehan grew lively.

—Let's have a squint at her, Corley, he said.

Corley glanced sideways at his friend and an unpleasant grin appeared on his face.

—Are you trying to get inside me? he asked.

—Damn it! said Lenehan boldly, I don't want an introduction. All I want is to have a look at her. I'm not going to eat her.

—O ... A look at her? said Corley, more amiably. Well ... I'll tell you what. I'll go over and talk to her and you can pass by.

—Right! said Lenehan.

Corley had already thrown one leg over the chains when Lenehan called out:

—And after? Where will we meet?

—Half ten, answered Corley, bringing over his other leg.

—Where?

—Corner of Merrion Street. We'll be coming back.

—Work it all right now, said Lenehan in farewell.

Corley did not answer. He sauntered across the road swaying his head from side to side. His bulk, his easy pace and the solid sound of his boots had something of the conqueror in them. He approached the young woman and, without saluting, began at once to converse with her. She swung her sunshade more quickly and executed half turns on her heels. Once or twice when he spoke to her at close quarters she laughed and bent her head.

Lenehan observed them for a few minutes. Then he walked rapidly along beside the chains to some distance and crossed the road obliquely. As he approached Hume Street corner he found the air heavily scented and his eyes made a swift anxious scrutiny of the young woman's appearance. She had her Sunday finery on. Her blue serge skirt was held at the waist by a belt of black leather. The great silver buckle of her belt seemed to depress the centre of her body, catching the light stuff of her white blouse like a clip. She wore a short black jacket with mother-of-pearl buttons and a ragged black boa. The ends of her tulle collarette had been carefully disordered and a big bunch of red flowers was pinned in her bosom, stems upwards. Lenehan's eyes noted approvingly her stout short muscular body. Frank rude health glowed in her face, on her fat red cheeks and in her unabashed blue eyes. Her features were blunt. She had broad nostrils, a straggling mouth which lay open in a contented leer, and two projecting front teeth. As he passed Lenehan took off his cap and, after about ten seconds, Corley returned a salute to the air. This he did by raising his hand vaguely and pensively changing the angle of position of his hat.

Lenehan walked as far as the Shelbourne Hotel where he halted and waited. After waiting for a little time he saw them coming towards him and, when they turned to the right, he followed them, stepping lightly in his white shoes, down one side of Merrion Square. As he walked on slowly, timing his pace to theirs, he watched Corley's head which turned at every moment towards the young woman's face like a big ball revolving on a pivot. He kept the pair in view until he had seen them climbing the stairs of the Donnybrook tram; then he turned about and went back the way he had come.

Now that he was alone his face looked older. His gaiety seemed to forsake him and, as he came by the railings of the Duke's Lawn, he allowed his hand to run along them. The air which the harpist had played began to control his movements. His softly padded feet played the melody while his fingers swept a scale of variations idly along the railings after each group of notes.

He walked listlessly round Stephen's Green and then down Grafton Street. Though his eyes took note of many elements of the crowd through which he passed they did so morosely. He found trivial all that was meant to charm him and did not answer the glances which invited him to be bold. He knew that he would have to speak a great deal, to invent and to amuse, and his brain and throat were too dry for such a task. The problem of how he could pass the hours till he met Corley again troubled him a little. He could think of no way of passing them but to keep on walking. He turned to the left when he came to the corner of Rutland Square and felt more at ease in the dark quiet street, the sombre look of which suited his mood. He paused at last before the window of a poor-looking shop over which the words *Refreshment Bar* were printed in white letters. On the glass of the window were two flying inscriptions: *Ginger Beer* and *Ginger Ale*. A cut ham was exposed on a great blue dish while near it on a plate lay a segment of very light plum-pudding. He eyed this food earnestly for some time and then, after glancing warily up and down the street, went into the shop quickly.

He was hungry for, except some biscuits which he had asked two grudging curates to bring him, he had eaten nothing since breakfast-time. He sat down at an uncovered wooden table opposite two work-girls and a mechanic. A slatternly girl waited on him.

—How much is a plate of peas? he asked.

—Three halfpence, sir, said the girl.

—Bring me a plate of peas, he said, and a bottle of ginger beer.

He spoke roughly in order to belie his air of gentility for his entry had been followed by a pause of talk. His face was heated. To appear natural he pushed his cap back on his head and planted his elbows on the table. The mechanic and the two work-girls examined him point by point before resuming their conversation in a subdued voice. The girl brought him a plate of hot grocer's peas, seasoned with pepper and vinegar, a fork and his ginger beer. He ate his food greedily and found it so good that he made a note of the shop mentally. When he had eaten all the peas he sipped his ginger beer and sat for some time thinking of Corley's adventure. In his imagination he beheld the pair of lovers walking along some dark road; he heard Corley's voice in deep energetic gallantries and saw again the leer of the young woman's mouth. This vision made him feel keenly his own poverty of purse and spirit. He was tired of knocking about, of pulling the devil by the tail, of shifts and intrigues. He would be thirty-one in November. Would he never get a good job? Would he never have a home of his own? He thought how pleasant it would be to have a warm fire to sit by and a good dinner to sit down to. He had walked the streets long enough with friends and with girls. He knew what those friends were worth: he knew the girls too. Experience had embittered his heart against the world. But all hope had not left him. He felt better after having eaten than he had felt before, less weary of his life, less vanquished in spirit. He might yet be able to settle down in some snug corner and live happily if he could only come across some good simple-minded girl with a little of the ready.

He paid twopence halfpenny to the slatternly girl and went out of the shop to begin his wandering again. He went into Capel Street and walked along towards the City Hall. Then he turned into Dame Street. At the corner of

George's Street he met two friends of his and stopped to converse with them. He was glad that he could rest from all his walking. His friends asked him had he seen Corley and what was the latest. He replied that he had spent the day with Corley. His friends talked very little. They looked vacantly after some figures in the crowd and sometimes made a critical remark. One said that he had seen Mac an hour before in Westmoreland Street. At this Lenehan said that he had been with Mac the night before in Egan's. The young man who had seen Mac in Westmoreland Street asked was it true that Mac had won a bit over a billiard match. Lenehan did not know: he said that Holohan had stood them drinks in Egan's.

He left his friends at a quarter to ten and went up George's Street. He turned to the left at the City Markets and walked on into Grafton Street. The crowd of girls and young men had thinned and on his way up the street he heard many groups and couples bidding one another good-night. He went as far as the clock of the College of Surgeons: it was on the stroke of ten. He set off briskly along the northern side of the Green, hurrying for fear Corley should return too soon. When he reached the corner of Merrion Street he took his stand in the shadow of a lamp and brought out one of the cigarettes which he had reserved and lit it. He leaned against the lamp-post and kept his gaze fixed on the part from which he expected to see Corley and the young woman return.

His mind became active again. He wondered had Corley managed it successfully. He wondered if he had asked her yet or if he would leave it to the last. He suffered all the pangs and thrills of his friend's situation as well as those of his own. But the memory of Corley's slowly revolving head calmed him somewhat: he was sure Corley would pull it off all right. All at once the idea struck him that perhaps Corley had seen her home by another way and given him the slip. His eyes searched the street: there was no sign of them. Yet it was surely half-an-hour since he had seen the clock of the College of Surgeons. Would Corley do a thing like that? He lit his last cigarette and began to smoke it nervously. He strained his eyes as each tram stopped at the far corner of the square. They must have gone home by another way. The paper of his cigarette broke and he flung it into the road with a curse.

Suddenly he saw them coming towards him. He started with delight and, keeping close to his lamp-post, tried to read the result in their walk. They were walking quickly, the young woman taking quick short steps, while Corley kept beside her with his long stride. They did not seem to be speaking. An intimation of the result pricked him like the point of a sharp instrument. He knew Corley would fail; he knew it was no go.

They turned down Baggot Street and he followed them
at once, taking the other footpath. When they stopped
he stopped too. They talked for a few moments and then
the young woman went down the steps into the area of a
house. Corley remained standing at the edge of the path, a
little distance from the front steps. Some minutes passed.
Then the hall-door was opened slowly and cautiously. A
woman came running down the front steps and coughed.
Corley turned and went towards her. His broad figure hid
hers from view for a few seconds and then she reappeared
running up the steps. The door closed on her and Corley
began to walk swiftly towards Stephen's Green.

Lenehan hurried on in the same direction. Some drops
of light rain fell. He took them as a warning and, glancing back towards the house which the young woman had
entered to see that he was not observed, he ran eagerly
across the road. Anxiety and his swift run made him pant.
He called out:

—Hallo, Corley!

Corley turned his head to see who had called him, and
then continued walking as before. Lenehan ran after him,
settling the waterproof on his shoulders with one hand.

—Hallo, Corley! he cried again.

He came level with his friend and looked keenly in his
face. He could see nothing there.

—Well? he said. Did it come off?

They had reached the corner of Ely Place. Still without answering Corley swerved to the left and went up the side street. His features were composed in stern calm. Lenehan kept up with his friend, breathing uneasily. He was baffled and a note of menace pierced through his voice.

—Can't you tell us? he said. Did you try her?

Corley halted at the first lamp and stared grimly before him. Then with a grave gesture he extended a hand towards the light and, smiling, opened it slowly to the gaze of his disciple. A small gold coin shone in the palm.

The Sniper

Liam O'Flaherty

The long June twilight faded into night. Dublin lay enveloped in darkness, but for the dim light of the moon, that shone through fleecy clouds, casting a pale light as of approaching dawn over the streets and the dark waters of the Liffey. Around the beleaguered Four Courts the heavy guns roared. Here and there through the city machine guns and rifles broke the silence of the night, spasmodically, like dogs barking on lone farms. Republicans and Free Staters were waging civil war.

On a roof-top near O'Connell Bridge, a Republican sniper lay watching. Beside him lay his rifle and over his shoulders were slung a pair of field-glasses. His face was the face of a student, thin and ascetic, but his eyes had the cold gleam of a fanatic. They were deep and thoughtful, the eyes of a man who is used to looking at death.

He was eating a sandwich hungrily. He had eaten nothing since morning. He had been too excited to eat. He finished the sandwich, and taking a flask of whiskey from his pocket, he took a short draught. Then he returned the flask to his pocket. He paused for a moment, considering whether he should risk a smoke. It was dangerous. The flash might be seen in the darkness and there were enemies watching. He decided to take the risk. Placing a cigarette between his lips, he struck a match, inhaled the smoke hurriedly and put out the light. Almost immediately a bullet flattened itself against the parapet of the roof. The sniper took another whiff and put out the cigarette. Then he swore softly and crawled away to the left.

Cautiously he raised himself and peered over the parapet. There was a flash and a bullet whizzed over his head. He dropped immediately. He had seen the flash. It came from the opposite side of the street.

He rolled over the roof to a chimney stack in the rear, and slowly drew himself up behind it, until his eyes were level with the top of the parapet. There was nothing to be seen—just the dim outline of the opposite housetop against the blue sky. His enemy was under cover.

Just then an armoured car came across the bridge and advanced slowly up the street. It stopped on the opposite side of the street fifty yards ahead. The sniper could hear the dull panting of the motor. His heart beat faster. It was an enemy car. He wanted to fire, but he knew it was useless. His bullets would never pierce the steel that covered the grey monster.

Then round the corner of a side street came an old woman, her head covered by a tattered shawl. She began to talk to the man in the turret of the car. She was pointing to the roof where the sniper lay. An informer.

The turret opened. A man's head and shoulders appeared, looking towards the sniper. The sniper raised his rifle and fired. The head fell heavily on the turret wall. The woman darted toward the side street. The sniper fired again. The woman whirled round and fell with a shriek into the gutter.

Suddenly from the opposite roof a shot rang out and the sniper dropped his rifle with a curse. The rifle clattered to the roof. The sniper thought the noise would wake the dead. He stopped to pick the rifle up. He couldn't lift it. His forearm was dead. 'Christ,' he muttered, 'I'm hit.'

Dropping flat on the roof, he crawled back to the parapet. With his left hand he felt the injured right forearm. The blood was oozing through the sleeve of his coat. There was no pain—just a deadened sensation, as if the arm had been cut off.

Quickly he drew his knife from his pocket, opened it on the breastwork of the parapet and ripped open the sleeve. There was a small hole where the bullet had entered. On the other side there was no hole. The bullet had lodged in the bone. It must have fractured it. He bent the arm below the wound. The arm bent back easily. He ground his teeth to overcome the pain.

Then, taking out his field dressing, he ripped open the packet with his knife. He broke the neck of the iodine bottle and let the bitter fluid drip into the wound. A paroxysm of pain swept through him. He placed the cotton wadding over the wound and wrapped the dressing over it. He tied the end with his teeth.

Then he lay still against the parapet, and closing his eyes, he made an effort of will to overcome the pain.

In the street beneath all was still. The armoured car had retired speedily over the bridge, with the machine gunner's head hanging lifeless over the turret. The woman's corpse lay still in the gutter.

The sniper lay still for a long time nursing his wounded arm and planning escape. Morning must not find him wounded on the roof. The enemy on the opposite roof covered his escape. He must kill that enemy and he could not use his rifle. He had only a revolver to do it. Then he thought of a plan.

Taking off his cap, he placed it over the muzzle of his rifle. Then he pushed the rifle slowly upwards over the parapet, until the cap was visible from the opposite side of the street. Almost immediately there was a report, and a bullet pierced the centre of the cap. The sniper slanted the rifle forward. The cap slipped down into the street. Then, catching the rifle in the middle, the sniper dropped his left hand over the roof and let it hang, lifelessly. After a few moments he let the rifle drop to the street. Then he sank to the roof, dragging his hand with him.

Crawling quickly to the left, he peered up at the corner of the roof. His ruse had succeeded. The other sniper seeing the cap and rifle fall, thought that he had killed his man. He was now standing before a row of chimney pots, looking across, with his head clearly silhouetted against the western sky.

The Republican sniper smiled and lifted his revolver above the edge of the parapet. The distance was about fifty yards—a hard shot in the dim light, and his right arm was paining him like a thousand devils. He took a steady aim. His hand trembled with eagerness. Pressing his lips together, he took a deep breath through his nostrils and fired. He was almost deafened with the report and his arm shook with the recoil.

Then, when the smoke cleared, he peered across and uttered a cry of joy. His enemy had been hit. He was reeling over the parapet in his death agony. He struggled to keep his feet, but he was slowly falling forward, as if in a dream. The rifle fell from his grasp, hit the parapet, fell over, bounded off the pole of a barber's shop beneath and then clattered on to the pavement.

Then the dying man on the roof crumpled up and fell forward. The body turned over and over in space and hit the ground with a dull thud. Then it lay still.

The sniper looked at his enemy falling and he shuddered. Then lust of battle died in him. He became bitten by remorse. The sweat stood out in beads on his forehead. Weakened by his wound and the long summer day of fasting and watching on the roof, he revolted from the sight of the shattered mass of his dead enemy. His teeth chattered. He began to gibber to himself, cursing the war, cursing himself, cursing everybody.

He looked at the smoking revolver in his hand and with an oath he hurled it to the roof at his feet. The revolver went off with the concussion, and the bullet whizzed past the sniper's head. He was frightened back to his senses by the shock. His nerves steadied. The cloud of fear scattered from his mind and he laughed.

Taking the whiskey flask from his pocket, he emptied it at a draught. He felt reckless under the influence of the spirits. He decided to leave the roof and look for his company commander to report. Everywhere around was quiet. There was not much danger in going through the streets. He picked up his revolver and put it in his pocket. Then he crawled down through the sky-light to the house underneath.

When the sniper reached the laneway on the street level, he felt a sudden curiosity as to the identity of the enemy sniper whom he had killed. He decided that he was a good shot whoever he was. He wondered if he knew him. Perhaps he had been in his own company before the split in the army. He decided to risk going over to have a look at him. He peered around the corner into O'Connell Street. In the upper part of the street there was heavy firing, but around here all was quiet.

The sniper darted across the street. A machine gun tore up the ground around him with a hail of bullets, but he escaped. He threw himself downwards beside the corpse. The machine gun stopped.

Then the sniper turned over the dead body and looked into his brother's face.

Unwelcome Idea

Elizabeth Bowen

Along Dublin bay, on a sunny July morning, the public gardens along the Dalkey tramline look bright as a series of parasols. Chalk-blue sea appears at the end of the roads of villas turning downhill—but these are still the suburbs, not the seaside. In the distance, floating across the bay, buildings glitter out of the heat-haze on the neck to Howth, and Howth Head looks higher veiled. After inland Ballsbridge, the tram from Dublin speeds up; it zooms through the residential reaches with the gathering steadiness of a launched ship. Its red velvet seating accommodation is seldom crowded—its rival, the quicker bus, lurches ahead of it down the same road.

After Ballsbridge, the ozone smell of the bay sifts more and more through the smell of chimneys and pollen and the July-darkened garden trees as the bay and line converge. Then at a point you see the whole bay open—there are nothing but flats of grass and the sunk railway between the running tram and the still sea. An immense glaring reflection floods through the tram. When high terraces, backs to the tramline, shut out the view again, even their backs have a salted, marine air: their cotton window-blinds are pulled half down, crooked; here and there an inner door left open lets you see a flash of sea through a house. The weathered lions on gate posts ought to be dolphins. Red, low-lying villas have been fitted between earlier terraces, ornate, shabby, glassy hotels, bow-fronted mansions all built in the first place to stand up over spaces of grass. Looks from trams and voices from public gardens invade the old walled lawns with their grottos and weeping willows. Spit-and-polish alternates with decay. But stucco, slate and slate-fronts, blotched Italian pink-wash, dusty windows, lace curtains, and dolphin-lions seem to be the eternity of this tram route. Quite soon the modern will sag, chip, fade. Change leaves everything at the same level. Nothing stays bright but mornings.

The tram slides to stops for its not many passengers. The Blackrock bottleneck checks it, then the Dun Laoghaire. These are the shopping centres strung on the line: their animation congests them. Housewives with burnt bare arms out of their cotton dresses mass blinking and talking among the halted traffic, knocking their shopping-bags on each other's thighs. Forgotten Protestant ladies from 'rooms' near the esplanade stand squeezed between the kerb and the shops. A file of booted children threads its way through the crush, a nun at the head like a needle. Children by themselves curl their toes in their plimsoles and suck sweets and disregard everything. The goods stacked in the shops look very static and hot. Out from the tops of the shops on brackets stand a number of clocks. As though wrought up by the clocks the tram-driver smites his bell again and again, till the checked tram noses its way through.

By half-past eleven this morning one tram to Dalkey is not far on its way. All the time it approaches the Ballsbridge stop Mrs Kearney looks undecided, but when it does pull up she steps aboard because she has seen no bus. In a slither of rather ungirt parcels, including a dress-box, with a magazine held firmly between her teeth, she clutches her way up the stairs to the top. She settles herself on a velvet seat: she is hot. But the doors at each end and the windows are half-open, and as the tram moves air rushes smoothly through. There are only four other people and no man smokes a pipe. Mrs Kearney has finished wedging her parcels between her hip and the sides of the tram and is intending to look at her magazine when she stares hard ahead and shows interest in someone's back. She moves herself and everything three seats up, leans forward and gives a poke at the back. 'Isn't that you?' she says.

Miss Kevin jumps round so wholeheartedly that the brims of the two hats almost clash. 'Why, for goodness' sake! ... Are you on the tram?' She settled round in her seat with her elbow hooked over the back—it is bare and sharp, with a rubbed joint: she and Mrs Kearney are of an age, and the age is about thirty-five. They both wear printed dresses that in this weather stick close to their backs; they are enthusiastic, not close friends but as close as they are ever likely to be. They both have high, fresh, pink colouring; Mrs Kearney could do with a little less weight and Miss Kevin could do with a little more.

They agree they are out early. Miss Kevin has been in town for the July sales but is now due home to let her mother go out. She has parcels with her but they are compact and shiny, having been made up at the counters of shops. 'They all say, buy now. You never know.' She cannot help looking at Mrs Kearney's parcels, bursting out from their string. 'And aren't you very laden, also,' she says.

'I tell you what I've been doing,' says Mrs Kearney. 'I've been saying goodbye to my sister Maureen in Ballsbridge, and who knows how long it's to be for! My sister's off to

County Cavan this morning with the whole of her family and the maid.'

'For goodness' sake,' says Miss Kevin. 'Has she relatives there?'

'She has, but it's not that. She's evacuating. For the holidays they always go to Tramore, but this year she says she should evacuate.' This brings Mrs Kearney's parcels into the picture. 'So she asked me to keep a few of her things for her.' She does not add that Maureen has given her these old things, including the month-old magazine.

'Isn't it well for her,' says Miss Kevin politely. 'But won't she find it terribly slow down there?'

'She will, I tell you,' says Mrs Kearney. 'However, they're all driving down in the car. She's full of it. She says we should all go somewhere where we don't live. It's nothing to her to shift when she has the motor. But the latest thing I hear they say now in the paper is that we'll be shot if we don't stay where we are. They say now we're all to keep off the roads—and there's my sister this morning with her car at the door. Do you think they'll halt her, Miss Kevin?'

'They might,' says Miss Kevin. 'I hear they're very suspicious. I declare, with the instructions changing so quickly it's better to take no notice. You'd be upside down if you tried to follow them all. It's of the first importance to keep calm, they say, and however would we keep calm doing this, then that? Still, we don't get half the instructions they get in England. I should think they'd really pity themselves … Have you earth in your house, Mrs Kearney? We have, we have three buckets. The warden's delighted with us: he says we're models. We haven't a refuge, though. Have you one?'

'We have a kind of pump, but I don't know it is much good. And nothing would satisfy Fergus till he turned out the cellar.'

'Well, you're very fashionable!'

'The contents are on the lawn, and the lawn's ruined. He's crazy,' she says glumly, 'with ARP.'

'Aren't men very thorough,' says Miss Kevin with a virgin detachment that is rather annoying. She has kept thumbing her sales parcels, and now she cannot resist undoing one. 'Listen,' she says, 'isn't this a pretty delaine?' She runs the end of a fold between her finger and thumb. 'It drapes sweetly. I've enough for a dress and a bolero. It's French: they say we won't get any more now.'

'And that Coty scent—isn't that French?'

Their faces flood with the glare struck from the sea as the tram zooms smoothly along the open reach—wall and trees on its inland side, grass and bay on the other. The tips of their shingles and the thoughts in their heads are for the minute blown about and refreshed. Mrs Kearney flutters in the holiday breeze, but Miss Kevin is looking inside her purse. Mrs Kearney thinks she will take the kids to the strand. 'Are you a great swimmer, Miss Kevin?'

'I don't care for it: I've bad circulation. It's a fright to see me go blue. They say now the sea's full of mines,' she says, with a look at the great, innocent bay.

'Ah, they're tethered; they'd never bump you.'

'I'm not nervous at any time, but I take a terrible chill.'

'My sister Maureen's nervous. At Tramore she'll never approach the water: it's the plage she enjoys. I wonder what will she do if they stop the car—she has all her plate with her in the back with the maid. And her kiddies are very nervous: they'd never stand it. I wish now I'd asked her to send me a telegram. Or should I telegraph her to know did she arrive? ... Wasn't it you said we had to keep off the roads?'

'That's in the event of invasion, Mrs Kearney. In the event of not it's correct to evacuate.'

'She's correct all right, then,' says Mrs Kearney, with a momentary return to gloom. 'And if nothing's up by the finish she'll say she went for the holiday, and I shouldn't wonder if she still went to Tramore. Still, I'm sure I'm greatly relieved to hear what you say ... Is that your father's opinion?'

Miss Kevin becomes rather pettish. 'Him?' she says, 'oh gracious, I'd never ask him. He has great contempt for the whole war. My mother and I daren't refer to it—isn't it very mean of him? He does nothing but read the papers and roar away to himself. And will he let my mother or me near him when he has the news on? You'd think,' Miss Kevin says with a clear laugh, 'that the two of us originated the war to spite him: he doesn't seem to blame Hitler at all. He's really very unreasonable when he's not well. We'd a great fight to get in the buckets of earth, and now he makes out they're only there for the cat. And to hear the warden praising us makes him sour. Isn't it very mean to want us out of it all, when they say the whole country is drawn together? He doesn't take any pleasure in the ARP.'

'To tell you the truth I don't either,' says Mrs Kearney. 'Isn't it that stopped the Horse Show? Wouldn't that take the heart out of you—isn't that a great blow to national life? I never yet missed a Horse Show—Sheila was nearly born there. And isn't that a terrible blow to trade? I haven't the heart to look for a new hat. To my mind this war's getting very monotonous: all the interest of it is confined to a few ... Did you go to the Red Cross Fête?'

The tram glides to a halt in Dun Laoghaire Street. Simultaneously Miss Kevin and Mrs Kearney move up to the window ends of their seats and look closely down on the shop windows and shoppers. Town heat comes off the street in a quiver and begins to pervade the immobile tram. 'I declare to goodness,' exclaims Miss Kevin, 'there's my same delaine! French, indeed! And watch the figure it's on—it would sicken you.'

But with parallel indignation Mrs Kearney has just noticed a clock. 'Will you look at the time!' she says, plaintively. 'Isn't this an awfully slow tram! There's my morning gone, and not a thing touched at home, from attending evacuations. It's well for her! She expected me on her step by ten—"It's a terrible parting," she says on the p.c.[1] But all she does at the last is to chuck the parcels at me, then keep me running to see had they the luncheon basket and what had they done with her fur coat ... I'll be off at the next stop, Miss Kevin dear. Will you tell your father and mother I was asking inquiring for them?' Crimson again at the very notion of moving, she begins to scrape her parcels under her wing. 'Well,' she says, 'I'm off with the *objets d'art*.' The heels of a pair of evening slippers protrude from a gap at the end of the dress-box. The tram-driver, by smiting his bell, drowns any remark Miss Kevin could put out: the tram clears the crowd and moves down Dun Laoghaire Street, between high flights of steps, lace curtains, gardens with round beds. 'Bye-bye, now,' says Mrs Kearney, rising and swaying.

'Bye-bye to you,' said Miss Kevin. 'Happy days to us all.'

Mrs Kearney, near the top of the stairs, is preparing to bite on the magazine. 'Go on!' she says. 'I'll be seeing you before then.'

[1] Passenger car.

A Rhinoceros, Some Ladies, and a Horse

James Stephens

One day, in my first job, a lady fell in love with me. It was quite unreasonable, of course, for I wasn't wonderful: I was small and thin, and I weighed much the same as a largish duck-egg. I didn't fall in love with her, or anything like that. I got under the table, and stayed there until she had to go wherever she had to go to.

I had seen an advertisement—'Smart boy wanted,' it said. My legs were the smartest things about me, so I went there on the run. I got the job.

At that time there was nothing on God's earth that I could do, except run. I had no brains, and I had no memory. When I was told to do anything I got into such an enthusiasm about it that I couldn't remember anything else about it. I just ran as hard as I could, and then I ran back, proud and panting. And when they asked me for the whatever-it-was that I had run for, I started, right on the instant, and ran some more.

The place I was working at was, amongst other things, a theatrical agency. I used to be sitting in a corner of the office floor, waiting to be told to run somewhere and back. A lady would come in—a music-hall lady that is—and, in about five minutes, howls of joy would start coming from the inner office. Then, peacefully enough, the lady and my two bosses would come out, and the lady always said, 'Splits! I can do splits like no one.' And one of my bosses would say, 'I'm keeping your splits in mind.' And the other would add, gallantly—'No one who ever saw your splits could ever forget 'em.'

One of my bosses was thin, and the other was fat. My fat boss was composed entirely of stomachs. He had three baby-stomachs under his chin: then he had three more descending in even larger englobings nearly to the ground: but, just before reaching the ground, the final stomach bifurcated into a pair of boots. He was very light on these and could bounce about in the neatest way.

He was the fattest thing I had ever seen, except a rhinoceros that I had met in the Zoo the Sunday before I got the job. That rhino was *very* fat, and it had a smell like twenty-five pigs. I was standing outside its palisade, wondering what it could possibly feel like to be a rhinoceros, when two larger boys passed by. Suddenly they caught hold of me, and pushed me through the bars of the palisade. I was very skinny, and in about two seconds I was right inside, and the rhinoceros was looking at me.

It was very fat, but it wasn't fat like stomachs, it was fat like barrels of cement, and when it moved it creaked a lot, like a woman I used to know who creaked like an old bedstead. The rhinoceros swaggled over to me with a bunch of cabbage sticking out of its mouth. It wasn't angry, or anything like that, it just wanted to see who I was. Rhinos are blindish: they mainly see by smelling, and they smell in snorts. This one started at my left shoe, and snorted right up that side of me to my ear. He smelt that very carefully: then he switched over to my right ear, and snorted right down that side of me to my right shoe: then he fell in love with my shoes and began to lick them. I, naturally, wriggled my feet at that, and the big chap was so astonished that he did the strangest step-dance backwards to his pile of cabbages, and began to eat them.

I squeezed myself out of his cage and walked away. In a couple of minutes I saw the two boys. They were very frightened, and they asked me what I had done to the rhinoceros. I answered, a bit grandly, perhaps, that I had seized it in both hands, ripped it limb from limb, and tossed its carcase to the crows. But when they began shouting to people that I had just murdered a rhinoceros I took to my heels, for I didn't want to be arrested and hanged for a murder that I hadn't committed.

Still, a man can't be as fat as a rhinoceros, but my boss was as fat as a man can be. One day a great lady of the halls came in, and was received on the knee. She was very great. Her name was Maudie Darling, or thereabouts. My bosses called her nothing but 'Darling', and she called them the same. When the time came for her to arrive the whole building got palpitations of the heart. After waiting a while my thin boss got angry, and said—'Who does the woman think she is? If she isn't here in two twos I'll go down to the entry, and when she does come I'll boot her out.' The fat boss said—'She's only two hours late, she'll be here before the week's out.'

Within a few minutes there came great clamours from the courtyard. Patriotic cheers, such as Parnell himself never got, were thundering. My bosses ran instantly to the inner office. Then the door opened, and the lady appeared.

She was very wide, and deep, and magnificent. She was dressed in camels and zebras and goats: she had two peacocks in her hat and a rabbit muff in her hand, and she strode among these with prancings.

But when she got right into the room and saw herself being looked at by three men and a boy she became adorably shy: one could see that she had never been looked at before.

'O,' said she, with a smile that made three and a half hearts beat like one, 'O,' said she, very modestly, 'is Mr Which-of-'em-is-it really in? Please tell him that Little-Miss-Me would be so glad to see and to be—'

Then the inner door opened, and the large lady was surrounded by my fat boss and my thin boss. She crooned to them—'O, you dear boys, you'll never know how much I've thought of you and longed to see you.'

That remark left me stupefied. The first day I got to the office I heard that it was the fat boss's birthday, and that he was thirty years of age: and the thin boss didn't look a day younger than the fat one. How the lady could mistake these old men for boys seemed to me the strangest fact that had ever come my way. My own bet was that they'd both die of old age in about a month.

After a while they all came out again. The lady was helpless with laughter: she had to be supported by my two bosses—'O,' she cried, 'you boys will kill me.' And the bosses laughed and laughed, and the fat one said— 'Darling, you're a scream,' and the thin one said—'Darling, you're a riot.'

And then ... she saw me! I saw her seeing me the very way I had seen the rhinoceros seeing me: I wondered for an instant would she smell me down one leg and up the other. She swept my two bosses right away from her, and she became a kind of queen, very glorious to behold: but sad, startled. She stretched a long, slow arm out and out and then she unfolded a long, slow finger, and pointed it at me—'Who is THAT??' she whispered in a strange whisper that could be heard two miles off.

My fat boss was an awful liar—'The cat brought that in,' said he.

But the thin boss rebuked him: 'No,' he said, 'it was not the cat. Let me introduce you; darling, this is James. James, this is the darling of the gods.'

'And of the pit,' said she, sternly.

She looked at me again. Then she sank to her knees and spread out both arms to me.

'Come to my boozalum, angel,' said she in a tender kind of way.

I knew what she meant, and I knew that she didn't know how to pronounce that word. I took a rapid glance at the area indicated. The lady had a boozalum you could graze a cow on. I didn't wait one second, but slid, in one swift, silent slide, under the table. Then she came forward and said a whole lot of poems to me under the table, imploring me, among a lot of odd things, to 'come forth, and gild the morning with my eyes', but at last she was reduced to whistling at me with two fingers in her mouth, the way you whistle for a cab.

I learned after she had gone that most of the things she said to me were written by a poet fellow named Spokeshave. They were very complimentary, but I couldn't love a woman who mistook my old bosses for boys, and had a boozalum that it would take an Arab chieftain a week to trot across on a camel.

The thin boss pulled me from under the table by my leg, and said that my way was the proper way to treat a rip, but my fat boss said, very gravely—'James, when a lady invites a gentleman to her boozalum a real gentleman hops there as pronto as possible, and I'll have none but real gentlemen in this office.'

'Tell me,' he went on, 'what made that wad of Turkish Delight fall in love with you?'

'She didn't love me at all, sir,' I answered.

'No?' he inquired.

'She was making fun of me,' I explained.

'There's something in that,' said he seriously, and went back to his office.

I had been expecting to be sacked that day. I was sacked the next day, but that was about a horse.

I had been given three letters to post, and told to run or they'd be too late. So I ran to the post office and round it and back, with, naturally, the three letters in my pocket. As I came to our door a nice, solid, red-faced man rode up on a horse. He thrust the reins into my hand—

'Hold the horse for a minute,' said he.

'I can't,' I replied, 'my boss is waiting for me.'

'I'll only be a minute,' said he angrily, and he walked off.

Well, there was I, saddled, as it were, with a horse. I looked at it, and it looked at me. Then it blew a pint of soap-suds out of its nose and took another look at me, and then the horse fell in love with me as if he had just found his long-lost foal. He started to lean against me and to woo me with small whinneys, and I responded and replied as best I could.

'Don't move a toe,' said I to the horse, 'I'll be back in a minute.'

He understood exactly what I said, and the only move he made was to swing his head and watch me as I darted up the street. I was less than half a minute away anyhow, and never out of his sight.

Up the street there was a man, and sometimes a woman, with a barrow, thick-piled with cabbages and oranges and apples. As I raced round the barrow I pinched an apple off it at full speed, and in ten seconds I was back at the horse. The good nag had watched every move I made, and when I got back his eyes were wide open, his mouth was wide open, and he had his legs splayed out so that he couldn't possibly slip. I broke the apple in halves and popped one half into his mouth. He ate it in slow crunches, and then he looked diligently at the other half. I gave him the other half, and, as he ate it, he gurgled with cidery gargles of pure joy. He then swung his head round from me and pointed his nose up the street, right at the apple-barrow.

I raced up the street again, and was back within the half-minute with another apple. The horse had nigh finished the first half of it when a man who had come up said, thoughtfully—

'He seems to like apples, bedad!'

'He loves them,' said I.

And then, exactly at the speed of lightning, the man became angry, and invented bristles all over himself like a porcupine.

'What the hell do you mean,' he hissed, and then he bawled, 'by stealing my apples?'

I retreated a bit into the horse.

'I didn't steal your apples,' I said.

'You didn't!' he roared, and then he hissed. 'I saw you,' he hissed.

'I didn't steal them,' I explained, 'I pinched them.'

'Tell me that one again,' said he.

'If,' said I patiently, 'if I took the apples for myself that would be stealing.'

'So it would,' he agreed.

'But as I took them for the horse that's pinching.'

'Be dam, but!' said he. ''Tis a real argument,' he went on, staring at the sky. 'Answer me that one,' he demanded of himself, and he was a very stupor of intellection. 'I give it up,' he roared, 'you give me back my apples.'

I placed the half apple that was left into his hand, and he looked at it as if it was a dead frog.

'What'll I do with that?' he asked earnestly.

'Give it to the horse,' said I.

The horse was now prancing at him, and mincing at him, and making love at him. He pushed the half apple into the horse's mouth, and the horse mumbled it and watched him, and chewed it and watched him, and gurgled it and watched him.

'He does like his bit of apple,' said the man.

'He likes you too,' said I. 'I think he loves you.'

'It looks like it,' he agreed, for the horse was yearning at him, and its eyes were soulful.

'Let's get him another apple,' said I, and, without another word, we both pounded back to his barrow and each of us pinched an apple off it. We got one apple into the horse, and were breaking the second one when a woman said gently—

'Nice, kind, Christian gentlemen, feeding dumb animals—with my apples,' she yelled suddenly.

The man with me jumped as if he had been hit by a train.

'Mary,' said he humbly.

'Joseph,' said she in a completely unloving voice.

But the woman transformed herself into nothing else but woman—

'What about my apples?' said she. 'How many have we lost?'

'Three,' said Joseph.

'Four,' said I, 'I pinched three and you pinched one.'

'That's true,' said he. 'That's exact, Mary. I only pinched one of our apples.'

'You only,' she squealed.

And I, hoping to be useful, broke in—

'Joseph,' said I, 'is the nice lady your boss?'

He halted for a dreadful second, and made up his mind.

'You bet she's my boss,' said he, 'and she's better than that, for she's the very wife of my bosom.'

She turned to me.

'Child of Grace—' said she—

Now, when I was a child, and did something that a woman didn't like she always expostulated in the same way. If I tramped on her foot, or jabbed her in the stomach—the way women have multitudes of feet and stomachs is always astonishing to a child—the remark such a woman made was always the same. She would grab her toe or her stomach, and say—'Childagrace, what the hell are you doing?' After a while I worked it out that Childagrace was one word, and was my name. When any woman in agony yelled Childagrace I ran right up prepared to be punished, and the woman always said tenderly, 'What are you yowling about, Childagrace.'

'Childagrace,' said Mary earnestly, 'how's my family to live if you steal our apples? You take my livelihood away from me! Very good, but will you feed and clothe and educate my children in,' she continued proudly, 'the condition to which they are accustomed?'

I answered that question cautiously.

'How many kids have you, ma'am?' said I.

'We'll leave that alone for a while,' she went on. 'You owe me two and six for the apples.'

'Mary!' said Joseph, in a pained voice.

'And you,' she snarled at him, 'owe me three shillings. I'll take it out of you in pints.' She turned to me.

'What do you do with all the money you get from the office here?'

'I give it to my landlady.'

'Does she stick to the lot of it?'

'Oh, no,' I answered, 'she always gives me back three-pence.'

'Well, you come and live with me and I'll give you back fourpence.'

'All right,' said I.

'By gum,' said Joseph, enthusiastically, 'that'll be fine. We'll go out every night and we won't steal a thing. We'll just pinch legs of beef, and pig's feet, and barrels of beer—'

'Wait now,' said Mary. 'You stick to your own landlady. I've trouble enough of my own. You needn't pay me the two and six.'

'Good for you,' said Joseph heartily, and then, to me—

'You just get a wife of your bosum half as kind as my wife of my bosum and you'll be set up for life. Mary,' he cried joyfully, 'let's go and have a pint on the strength of it.'

'You shut up,' said she.

'Joseph,' I interrupted, 'knows how to pronounce the word properly.'

'What word?'

'The one he used when he said you were the wife of his what-you-may-call-it.'

'I'm not the wife of any man's what-you-may-call-it,' said she, indignantly—'Oh, I see what you mean! So he pronounced it well, did he?'

'Yes, ma'am.'

She looked at me very sternly—

'How does it come you know about all these kinds of words?'

'Yes,' said Joseph, and he was even sterner than she was, 'when I was your age I didn't know any bad words.'

'A woman came into our office yesterday, and she mispronounced it.'

'What did she say now?'

'Oh, she said it all wrong.'

'Do you tell me so? We're all friends here: what way did she say it, son?'

'Well, ma'am, she called it a boozalum.'

'She said it wrong all right,' said Joseph, 'but 'tis a good, round, fat kind of a word all the same.'

'You shut up,' said Mary. 'Who did she say the word to?'

'She said it to me, ma'am.'

'She must have been a rip,' said Joseph.

'Was she a rip, now?'

'I don't know, ma'am. I never met a rip.'

'You're too young yet,' said Joseph, 'but you'll meet them later on. I never met a rip myself until I got married— I mean,' he added hastily, 'that they were all rips except the wife of my what-do-you-call-'ems, and that's why I married her.'

'I expect you've got a barrel-full of rips in your past,' she said bleakly, 'you must tell me about some of them tonight.' And then, to me, 'tell us about the woman,' said she.

So I told them all about her, and how she held out her arms to me, and said, 'Come to my boozalum, angel.'

'What did you do when she shoved out the old arms at you?' said Joseph.

'I got under the table,' I answered.

'That's not a bad place at all, but,' he continued earnestly, 'never get under the bed when there's an old girl chasing you, for that's the worst spot you could pick on. What was the strap's name?'

'Maudie Darling, she called herself.'

'You're a blooming lunatic,' said Joseph, 'she's the loveliest thing in the world, barring,' he added hastily, 'the wife of my blast-the-bloody-word.'

'We saw her last night,' said Mary, 'at Dan Lowrey's Theatre, and she's just lovely.'

'She isn't as nice as you, ma'am,' I asserted.

'Do you tell me that now?' said she.

'You are twice as nice as she is, and twenty times nicer.'

'There you are,' said Joseph, 'the very words I said to you last night.'

'You shut up,' said Mary scornfully, 'you were trying to knock a pint out of me! Listen, son,' she went on, 'we'll take all that back about your landlady. You come and live with me, and I'll give you back sixpence a week out of your wages.'

'All right, ma'am,' I crowed in a perfectly monstrous joy.

'Mary,' said Joseph, in a reluctant voice—

'You shut up,' said she.

'He can't come to live with us,' said Joseph. 'He's a bloody Prodestan,' he said sadly.

'Why—' she began—

'He'd keep me and the childer up all night, pinching apples for horses and asses, and reading the Bible, and up to every kind of devilment.'

Mary made up her mind quickly.

'You stick to your own landlady,' said she, 'tell her that I said she was to give you sixpence.' She whirled about. 'There won't be a thing left on that barrow,' said she to Joseph.

'Damn the scrap,' said Joseph violently.

'Listen,' said Mary to me very earnestly, 'am I nicer than Maudie Darling?'

'You are, ma'am,' said I.

Mary went down on the road on her knees: she stretched out both arms to me, and said—

'Come to my boozalum, angel.'

I looked at her, and I looked at Joseph, and I looked at the horse. Then I turned from them all and ran into the building and into the office. My fat boss met me—

'Here's your five bob,' said he. 'Get the hell out of here,' said he.

And I ran out.

I went to the horse, and leaned my head against the thick end of his neck, and the horse leaned as much of himself against me as he could manage. Then the man who owned the horse came up and climbed into his saddle. He fumbled in his pocket—

'You were too long,' said I. 'I've been sacked for minding your horse.'

'That's too bad,' said he: 'that's too damn bad,' and he tossed me a penny.

I caught it, and lobbed it back into his lap, and I strode down the street the most outraged human being then living in the world.

The Confirmation Suit

Brendan Behan

For weeks it was nothing but simony and sacrilege, and the sins crying to heaven for vengeance, the big green Catechism in our hands, walking home along the North Circular Road. And after tea, at the back of the brewery wall, with a butt too to help our wits, what is a pure spirit, and don't kill that, Billser has to get a drag out of it yet, what do I mean by apostate, and hell and heaven and despair and presumption and hope. The big fellows, who were now thirteen and the veterans of last year's Confirmation, frightened us, and said the Bishop would fire us out of the Chapel if we didn't answer his questions, and we'd be left wandering around the streets, in a new suit and topcoat with nothing to show for it, all dressed up and nowhere to go. The big people said not to mind them; they were only getting it up for us, jealous because they were over their Confirmation, and could never make it again. At school we were in a special room to ourselves, for the last few days, and went round, a special class of people. There were worrying times too, that the Bishop would light on you, and you wouldn't be able to answer his questions. Or you might hear the women complaining about the price of boys' clothes.

'Twenty-two and sixpence for tweed, I'd expect a share in the shop for that. I've a good mind to let him go in jersey and pants for that.'

'Quite right, ma'am,' says one to another, backing one another up, 'I always say what matter if they are good and pure.' What had that got to do with it, if you had to go into the Chapel in a jersey and pants, and every other kid in a new suit, kid gloves and tan shoes and a *scoil*[1] cap. The Cowan brothers were terrified. They were twins, and twelve years old, and every old one in the streets seemed to be wishing a jersey and pants on them, and saying their poor mother couldn't be expected to do for two in the one year, and she ought to go down to Sister Monica and tell her to put one back. If it came to that, the Cowans agreed to fight it out, at the back of the brewery wall; whoever got best, the other would be put back.

[1] Irish for 'school'.

I wasn't so worried about this. My old fellow was a tradesman, and made money most of the time. Besides, my grandmother, who lived at the top of the next house, was a lady of capernosity and function. She had money and lay in bed all day, drinking porter or malt, and taking pinches of snuff, and talking to the neighbours that would call up to tell her the news of the day. She only left her bed to go down one flight of stairs and visit the lady in the back drawing room, Miss McCann.

Miss McCann worked a sewing-machine, making habits for the dead. Sometimes girls from our quarter got her to make dresses and costumes, but mostly she stuck to the habits. They were a steady line, she said, and you didn't have to be always buying patterns, for the fashions didn't change, not even from summer to winter. They were like a long brown shirt, and a hood attached, that was closed over the person's face before the coffin lid was screwn down. A sort of little banner hung out of one arm, made of the same material, and four silk rosettes in each corner, and in the middle, the letters IHS, which mean, Miss McCann said, 'I Have Suffered'.

My grandmother and Miss McCann liked me more than any other kid they knew. I like being liked, and could only admire their taste.

My Aunt Jack, who was my father's aunt as well as mine, sometimes came down from where she lived, up near the Basin, where the water came from before they started getting it from Wicklow. My Aunt Jack said it was much better water, at that. Miss McCann said she ought to be a good judge. For Aunt Jack was funny. She didn't drink porter or malt, or take snuff, and my father said she never thought much about men either. She was also very strict about washing yourself very often. My grandmother took a bath every year, whether she was dirty or not, but she was in no way bigoted in the washing line in between times.

Aunt Jack made terrible raids on us now and again, to stop snuff and drink, and make my grandmother get up in the morning, and wash herself, and cook meals and take food with them. My grandmother was a gilder by trade, and served her time in one of the best shops in the city, and was getting a man's wages at sixteen. She liked stuff out of the pork butchers, and out of cans, but didn't like boiling potatoes, for she said she was no skivvy, and the chip man was better at it. When she was left alone it was a pleasure to eat with her. She always had cans of lovely things and spicy meat and brawn, and plenty of seasoning, fresh out of the German man's shop up the road. But after a visit from Aunt Jack, she would have to get up and wash for a week, and she would have to go and make stews and boil cabbage and pig's cheeks. Aunt Jack was very much up for sheep's heads too. They were so cheap and nourishing.

But my grandmother only tried it once. She had been a first-class gilder in Eustace Street, but never had anything to do with sheep's heads before. When she took it out of the pot, and laid it on the plate, she and I sat looking at it, in fear and trembling. It was bad enough going into the pot, but with the soup streaming from its eyes, and its big teeth clenched in a very bad temper, it would put the heart crossways in you. My grandmother asked me, in a whisper, if I ever thought sheep could look so vindictive, but that it was more like the head of an old man, and would I for God's sake take it up and throw it out of the window. The sheep kept glaring at us, but I came the far side of it, and rushed over to the window and threw it out in a flash. My grandmother had to drink a Baby Power whiskey, for she wasn't the better of herself.

Afterwards she kept what she called her stock-pot on the gas. A heap of bones and, as she said herself, any old muck that would come in handy, to have boiling there, night and day, on a glimmer. She and I ate happily of cooked ham and California pineapple and sock-eyes salmon, and the pot of good nourishing soup was always on the gas even if Aunt Jack came down the chimney, like the Holy Souls at midnight. My grandmother said she didn't begrudge the money for the gas. Not when she remembered the looks the sheep's head was giving her. And all she had to do with the stock-pot was throw in another sup of water, now and again, and a handful of old rubbish the pork butcher would send over, in the way of lights or bones. My Aunt Jack thought a lot about barley, too, so we had a package of that lying beside the gas, and threw a sprinkle in any time her foot was heard on the stairs. The stock-pot bubbled away on the gas for years after, and only when my grandmother was dead did someone notice it. They tasted it, and spat it out just as quick, and wondered what it was. Some said it was paste, and more that it was gold size, and there were other people and they maintained that it was glue. They all agreed on one thing, that it was dangerous tack to leave lying around where there might be young children, and in the heel of the reel, it went out the same window as the sheep's head.

Miss McCann told my grandmother not to mind Aunt Jack but to sleep as long as she liked in the morning. They came to an arrangement that Miss McCann would cover the landing and keep an eye out. She would call Aunt Jack in for a minute, and give the signal by banging the grate, letting on to poke the fire, and have a bit of a conversation with Aunt Jack about dresses and costumes, and hats and habits. One of these mornings, and Miss McCann delaying a fighting action, to give my grandmother time to hurl herself out of bed and into her clothes and give her face a rub of a towel, the chat between Miss McCann and Aunt Jack came to my Confirmation suit.

When I made my first Communion, my grandmother dug deep under the mattress, and myself and Aunt Jack were sent round expensive shops, and I came back with a rig that would take the sight of your eye. This time, however, Miss McCann said there wasn't much stirring in the habit line, on account of the mild winter, and she would be delighted to make the suit, if Aunt Jack would get the material. I nearly wept, for terror of what these old women would have me got up in, but I had to let on to be delighted, Miss McCann was so set on it. She asked Aunt Jack did she remember my father's Confirmation suit. *He* did. He said he would never forget it. They sent him out in a velvet suit, of plum colour, with a lace collar. My blood ran cold when he told me.

The stuff they got for my suit was blue serge, and that was not so bad. They got as far as the pants, and that passed off very civil. You can't do much to a boy's pants, one pair is like the next, though I had to ask them not to trouble themselves putting three little buttons on either side of the legs. The waistcoat was all right, and anyway the coat would cover it. But the coat itself, that was where Aughrim was lost.

The lapels were little wee things, like what you'd see in pictures like Ring magazine of John L. Sullivan or Gentleman Jim, and the buttons were the size of saucers, or within the bawl of an ass of it, and I nearly cried when

I saw them being put on, and ran down to my mother, and begged her to get me any sort of a suit, even a jersey and pants, than have me set up before the people in this get-up. My mother said it was very kind of Aunt Jack and Miss McCann to go to all this trouble and expense, and that I was very ungrateful not to appreciate it. My father said that Miss McCann was such a good tailor that people were dying to get into her creations, and her handiwork was to be found in all the best cemeteries. He laughed himself sick at this, and said if it was good enough for him to be sent down to North William Street in plum-coloured velvet and lace, I needn't be getting the needle over a couple of big buttons and little lapels. He asked me not forget to get up early the morning of my Confirmation, and let him see me, before he went to work: a bit of a laugh started the day well. My mother told him to give over and let me alone, and said she was sure it would be a lovely suit, and that Aunt Jack would never buy poor material, but stuff that would last forever. That nearly finished me altogether, and I ran through the hall up to the corner, fit to cry my eyes out, only I wasn't much of a hand at crying. I went more for cursing, and I cursed all belonging to me, and was hard at it on my father, and wondering why his lace collar hadn't choked him, when I remembered that it was a sin to go on like that, and I going up for Confirmation, and I had to simmer down, and live in fear of the day I'd put on that jacket.

The days passed, and I was fitted and refitted, and every old one in the house came up to look at the suit, and took a pinch of snuff, and a sup out of the jug, and wished me long life and the health to wear and tear it, and they spent that much time viewing it round, back, belly and sides, that Miss McCann hadn't time to make the overcoat, and like an answer to prayer, I was brought down to Talbot Street, and dressed out in a dinging overcoat, belted, like a grown-up man's. And my shoes and gloves were dear and dandy, and I said to myself that there was no need to let anyone see the suit with its little lapels and big buttons. I could keep the topcoat on all day in the Chapel and going round afterwards.

The night before Confirmation day, Miss McCann handed over the suit to my mother, and kissed me, and said not to bother thanking her. She would do more than that for me, and she and my grandmother cried and had a drink on the strength of my having grown to be a big fellow, in the space of twelve years, which they didn't seem to consider a great deal of time. My father said to my mother, and I getting bathed before the fire, that since I was born Miss McCann thought the world of me. When my mother was in hospital, she took me into her place till my mother came out, and it near broke her heart to give me back.

In the morning I got up, and Mrs Rooney in the next room shouted in to my mother that her Liam was still stalling, and not making any move to get out of it, and she thought she was cursed; Christmas or Easter, Communion or Confirmation, it would drive a body into Riddleys, which is the mad part of Grangegorman, and she wondered she wasn't driven out of her mind and above in the puzzle factory years ago. So she shouted again at Liam to get up and washed and dressed. And my mother shouted at me, though I was already knotting my tie, but you might as well be out of the world as out of fashion, and they kept it up like a pair of mad women, until at last Liam and I were ready and he came in to show my mother his clothes. She hanselled him a tanner which he put in his pocket and Mrs Rooney called me in to show her my clothes. I just stood at her door, and didn't open my coat, but just grabbed the sixpence out of her hand, and ran up the stairs like the hammers of hell. She shouted at me to hold on a minute, she hadn't seen my suit, but I muttered something about it not being lucky to keep a Bishop waiting, and ran on.

The Church was crowded, boys on one side and the girls on the other, and the altar ablaze with lights and flowers, and a throne for the Bishop to sit on when he wasn't confirming. There was a cheering crowd outside, drums rolled, trumpeters from Jim Larkin's band sounded the Salute. The Bishop came in and the doors were shut. In short order I joined the queue to the rails, knelt and was whispered over, and touched on the cheek. I had my overcoat on the whole time, though it was warm, and I was in a lather of sweat waiting for the hymns and the sermon.

The lights grew brighter and I got warmer, was carried out fainting. But though I didn't mind them loosening my tie, I clenched firmly my overcoat, and nobody saw the jacket with the big buttons and the little lapels. When I went home I got into bed, and my father said I went into a sickness just as the Bishop was giving us the pledge. He said this was a master stroke and showed real presence of mind.

Sunday after Sunday, my mother fought over the suit. She said I was a liar and a hypocrite, putting it on for a few minutes every week, and running into Miss McCann's and out again, letting her think I wore it every weekend. In a passionate temper my mother said she would show me up, and tell Miss McCann, and up like a shot with her, for my mother was always slim and light on her feet as a feather, and in next door. When she came back she said nothing, but sat at the fire looking into it. I didn't really believe she would tell Miss McCann. And I put on the suit and thought I would go in and tell her I was wearing it this weeknight, because I was going to the Queen's with my brothers. I ran next door and upstairs, and every step was more certain and easy that my mother hadn't told her. I ran, shoved in the door, saying: 'Miss Mc., Miss Mc., Rory and Sean and I are going to the Queen's ...' She was bent over the sewing-machine and all I could see was the top of her old grey head, and the rest of her shaking with crying, and her arms folded under her head, on a bit of habit where she had been finishing the IHS. I ran down the stairs and back into our place, and my mother was sitting at the fire, sad and sorry, but saying nothing.

I needn't have worried about the suit lasting forever. Miss McCann didn't. The next winter was not so mild, and she was whipped before the year was out. At her wake people said how she was in a habit of her own making, and my father said she would look queer in anything else, seeing as she supplied the dead of the whole quarter for forty years, without one complaint from a customer.

At the funeral, I left my topcoat in the carriage and got out and walked in the spills of rain after her coffin. People said I would get my end, but I went on till we reached the graveside, and I stood in my Confirmation suit drenched to the skin. I thought this was the least I could do.

Sierra Leone

John McGahern

'I suppose it won't be long now till your friend is here,' the barman said as he held the glass to the light after polishing.

'If it's not too wet,' I said.

'It's a bad evening,' he yawned, the rain drifting across the bandstand and small trees of Fairview Park to stream down the long window.

She showed hardly any signs of rain when she came, lifting the scarf from her black hair. 'You seem to have escaped the wet.' The barman was all smiles as he greeted her.

'I'm afraid I was a bit extravagant and took a taxi,' she said in the rapid speech she used when she was nervous or simulating confusion to create an effect.

'What would you like?'

'Would a hot whiskey be too much trouble?'

'No trouble at all.' The barman smiled and lifted the electric kettle. I moved the table to make room for her in the corner of the varnished partition beside the small coal fire in the grate. There was the sound of water boiling, and the scent of cloves and lemon. When I rose to go to the counter for the hot drink, the barman motioned that he would bring it over to the fire.

'The spoon is really to stop the glass from cracking'—I nodded towards the steaming glass in front of her on the table. It was a poor attempt to acknowledge the intimacy of the favour. For several months I had been frustrating all his attempts to get to know us, for we had picked Gaffneys because it was out of the way and we had to meet like thieves. Dublin was too small a city to give even our names away.

'This has just come.' I handed her the telegram as soon as the barman had resumed his polishing of the glasses. It was from my father, saying it was urgent I go home at once. She read it without speaking.

'What are you going to do?'

'I don't know. I suppose I'll have to go home.'

'It doesn't say *why*.'

'Of course not. He never gives room.'

'Is it likely to be serious?'

'No, but if I don't go there's the nagging doubt that it may be.'

'What are you going to do, then?'

'Go, I suppose.' I looked at her apprehensively.

'Then that's goodbye to our poor weekend,' she said.

We were the same age and had known each other casually for years. I had first met her with Jerry McCredy, a politician in his early fifties, who had a wife and family in the suburbs, and a reputation as a womanizer round the city; but by my time all the other women had disappeared. The black-haired Geraldine was with him everywhere, and he seemed to have fallen in love at last when old, even to the point of endangering his career. I had thought her young and lovely and wasted, but we didn't meet in any serious way till the night of the Cuban Crisis.

There was a general fever in the city that night, so quiet as to be almost unreal, the streets and faces hushed. I had been wandering from window to window in the area round Grafton Street. On every television set in the windows the Russian ships were still on course for Cuba. There was a growing air that we were walking in the last quiet evening of the world before it was all consumed by fire. 'It looks none too good.' I heard her quick laugh at my side as I stood staring at the ships moving silently across the screen.

'None too good.' I turned. 'Are you scared?'

'Of course I'm scared.'

'Do you know it's the first time we've ever met on our own?' I said. 'Where's Jerry?'

'He's in Cork. At a meeting. One that a loose woman like myself can't appear at.' She laughed her quick provocative laugh.

'Why don't you come for a drink, then?'

'I'd love to. With the way things are I was even thinking of going in for one on my own.'

There was a stillness in the bar such as I had never known. People looked up from their drinks as each fresh newsflash came on the set high in the corner, and it was with visible relief that they bent down again to the darkness of their pints.

'It's a real tester for that old chestnut about the Jesuit when he was asked what he'd do if he was playing cards at five minutes to midnight and was suddenly told that the world was going to end at midnight,' I said as I took our drinks to the table in one of the far corners of the bar, out of sight of the screen.

'And what would *he* do?'

'He'd continue playing cards, of course, to show that all things are equal. It's only love that matters.'

'That's a fine old farce.' She lifted her glass.

'It's strange, how I've always wanted to ask you out, and that it should happen this way. I always thought you very beautiful.'

'Why didn't you tell me?'

'You were with Jerry.'

'You should still have told me. I don't think Jerry ever minded the niceties very much when *he* was after a woman,' she laughed, and then added softly, 'Actually, I thought you disliked me.'

'Anyhow, we're here this night.'

'I know, but it's somehow hard to believe it.'

It was the stillness that was unreal, the comfortable sitting in chairs with drinks in our hands, the ships leaving a white wake behind them on the screen. We were in the condemned cell waiting for reprieve or execution, except that this time the whole world was the cell. There was nothing we could do. The withering would happen as simply as the turning on or off of a light bulb.

Her hair shone dark blue in the light. Her skin had the bloom of ripe fruit. The white teeth glittered when she smiled. We had struggled towards the best years; now they waited for us, and all was to be laid to waste as we were about to enter into them. In the freedom of the fear I moved my face close to hers. Our lips met. I put my hand on hers.

'Is Jerry coming back tonight?'

'No.'

'Can I stay with you tonight?'

'If you want that.' Her lips touched my face again.

'It's all I could wish for—except, maybe, a better time.'

'Why don't we go, then?' she said softly.

We walked by the Green, closed and hushed within its railings, not talking much. When she said, 'I wonder what they're doing in the Pentagon as we walk these steps by the Green?' it seemed more part of the silence than any speech.

'It's probably just as well we can't know.'

'I hope they do something. It'd be such a waste. All this to go, and us too.'

'We'd be enough.'

There was a bicycle against the wall of the hallway when she turned the key, and it somehow made the stairs and the lino-covered hallway more bare.

'It's the man's upstairs.' She nodded towards the bicycle. 'He works on the buses.'

The flat was small and untidy.

'I had always imagined Jerry kept you in more style,' I said idly.

'He doesn't keep me. I pay for this place. He always wanted me to move, but I would never give up my own place,' she said sharply, but she could not be harsh for long, and began to laugh. 'Anyhow he always leaves before morning. He has his breakfast in the other house;' and she switched off the light on the disordered bed and chairs and came into my arms. The night had been so tense and sudden that we had no desire except to lie in one another's arms, and as we kissed a last time before turning to seek our sleep she whispered, 'If you want me during the night, don't be afraid to wake me up.'

The Russian ships had stopped and were lying off Cuba, the radio told us as she made coffee on the small gas stove beside the sink in the corner of the room the next morning. The danger seemed about to pass. Again the world breathed, and it looked foolish to have believed it had ever been threatened.

Jerry was coming back from Cork that evening, and we agreed as we kissed to let this day go by without meeting but to meet at five the next day in Gaffneys of Fairview.

The bicycle had gone from the hallway by the time I had left. The morning met me as other damp cold Dublin mornings, the world almost restored already to the everyday. The rich uses we dreamed last night when it was threatened that we would put it to if spared were now forgotten, when again it lay all about us in such tedious abundance.

'Did Jerry notice or suspect anything?' I asked over the coal fire in Gaffneys when we met, both of us shy in our first meeting as separate persons after the intimacy of flesh.

'No. All he talked about was the Cuban business. Apparently, they were just as scared. They stayed up drinking all night in the hotel. He just had a terrible hangover.'

That evening we went to my room, and she was, in a calm and quiet way, completely free with her body, offering it as a gift, completely open. With the firelight leaping on the walls of the locked room, I said, 'There is no Cuba now. It is the first time, you and I,' but in my desire was too quick; 'I should have been able to wait,' but she took my face between her hands and drew it down. 'Don't worry. There will come a time soon enough when you won't have that trouble.'

'How did you meet Jerry?' I asked to cover the silence.

'My father was mixed up in politics in a small way and he was friendly with Jerry; and then my father died while I was at the convent in Eccles Street. Jerry seemed to do most of the arranging at the funeral, and it seemed natural for him to take me out on those halfdays and Sundays that we were given free.'

'Did you know of his reputation?'

'Everybody did. It made him dangerous and attractive. And one Saturday halfday we went to this flat in an attic off Baggot Street. He must have borrowed it for the occasion for I've never been in it since. I was foolish. I knew so little.

I just thought you lay in bed with a man and that was all that happened. I remember it was raining. The flat was right in the roof and there was the loud drumming of the rain all the time. That's how it began. And it's gone on from there ever since.'

She drew me towards her, in the full openness of desire, but she quickly rose. 'I have to hurry. I have to meet Jerry at nine'; and the pattern of her thieving had been set.

Often when I saw her dress to leave, combing her hair in the big cane armchair, drawing lipstick across her rich curving lips in the looking glass, I felt that she had come with stolen silver to the room. We had dined with the silver, and now that the meal was ended she was wiping and shining the silver anew, replacing it in the black jewel case to be taken out and used again in Jerry's bed or at his table, doubly soiled; and when I complained she said angrily, 'What about it? He doesn't know.'

'At least you and Jerry aren't fouling up anybody.'

'What about his wife? You seem very moral all of a sudden.'

'I'm sorry. I didn't mean to,' I apologized, but already the bloom had gone from the first careless fruits, and we felt the responsibility enter softly, but definitely, as any burden.

'Why can't you stay another hour?'

'I know what'd happen in one of those hours,' she said spiritedly, but the tone was affectionate and dreamy, perhaps with the desire for children. 'I'd get pregnant as hell.'

'What should we do?'

'Maybe we should tell Jerry,' she said. It was my turn to be alarmed.

'What would we tell him?'

The days of Jerry's profligacy were over. Not only had he grown jealous but violent. Not long before, hearing that she had been seen in a bar with a man and not being able to find her, he had taken a razor and slashed the dresses in her wardrobe to ribbons.

'We could tell him everything,' she said without conviction. 'That we want to be together.'

'He'd go berserk. You know that.'

'He's often said that the one thing he feels guilty about is having taken my young life. That we should have met when both of us were young.'

'That doesn't mean he'll think me the ideal man for the job,' I said. 'They say the world would be a better place if we looked at ourselves objectively and subjectively at others, but that's never the way the ball bounces.'

'Well, what are we to do?'

'By telling Jerry about us, you're just using one relationship to break up another. I think you should leave Jerry. Tell him that you just want to start up a life of your own.'

'But he'll know that there's someone.'

'That's his problem. You don't have to tell him. We can stay apart for a while. And then take up without any fear, like two free people.'

'I don't know,' she said as she put on her coat. 'And then, after all that, if I found out that you didn't want me, I'd be in a nice fix.'

'There'd be no fear of that. Where are you going tonight?'

'There's a dinner that a younger branch of the Party is giving. It's all right for me to go. They think it rather dashing of Jerry to appear with a young woman.'

'I'm not so sure. Young people don't like to see themselves caricatured either.'

'Anyhow I'm going,' she said.

'Will it be five in Gaffneys tomorrow?'

'At five, then,' I heard as the door opened and softly closed.

'Does Jerry suspect at all?' I asked her again another evening over Gaffneys' small coal fire.

'No. Not at all. Odd that he often was suspicious when nothing at all was going on and now that there is he suspects nothing. Only the other day he was asking about you. He was wondering what had become of you. It seemed so long since we had seen you last.'

Our easy thieving that was hardly loving, anxiety curbed by caution, appetite so luxuriously satisfied that it could not give way to the dreaming that draws us close to danger, was wearing itself naturally away when a different relationship was made alarmingly possible. Jerry was suddenly offered a lucrative contract to found a new radio/television network in Sierra Leone, and he was thinking of accepting. Ireland as a small nation with a history of oppression was suddenly becoming useful in the Third World.

'He goes to London the weekend after next for the interview and he'll almost certainly take it.'

'That means the end of his political career here.'

'There's not much further he can get here. It gives him prestige, a different platform, and a lot of cash.'

'How do you fit into this?'

'I don't know.'

'Does he want to take you with him?'

'He'll go out on his own first, but he says that as soon as he's settled there and sees the state of play that he wants me to follow him.'

'What'll you do?'

'I don't know,' she said in a voice that implied that I was now a part of these considerations.

Slane was a lovely old village in the English style close to Dublin. One Sunday we had lunch at the one hotel, more like a village inn than a hotel, plain wooden tables and chairs, the walls and fireplaces simple black and white, iron scrapers on the steps outside the entrance. She had suggested that we go there the weekend Jerry was on interview in London. The country weekend, the walks along the wooded banks of the river, coming back to the hotel with sharp appetites to have one drink in the bar and then to linger over lunch, in the knowledge that we had the whole long curtained afternoon spread before us, was dream enough. But was it to be that simple? Did we know one another outside the carnal pleasures we shared, and were we prepared to spend our lives together in the good or nightmare they might bring? It was growing clearer that she wasn't sure of me and that I wasn't sure. So when the telegram came from the country I was almost glad of the usual drama and mysteriousness.

'Then that's goodbye to our poor weekend.' She handed me back the telegram in Gaffneys.

'It's only one weekend,' I protested. 'We'll have as many as we want once Jerry goes.'

'You remember when I wanted to tell Jerry that we were in love and you wouldn't have it? You said we didn't know one another well enough, and then when we can have two whole days together you get this telegram. How are we ever going to get to know one another except by being together?'

'Maybe we can still go?'

'No. Not if you are doubtful. I think you should go home.'

'Will you come back with me this evening?'

'I have to have dinner with Jerry.'

'When?'

'At eight.'

'We'll have time. We can take a taxi.'

'No, love.' She was quite definite.

'Will you meet me when I come back, then?' I asked uncertainly.

'Jerry comes back from London on Sunday.'

'On Monday, then?'

'All right, on Monday.' There was no need to say where or when. She even said, 'See you Monday,' to the barman's silent inquiry as we left, and he waved 'Have a nice weekend,' as he gathered in our glasses.

I was returning home: a last look at the telegram before throwing it away—an overnight bag, the ticket, the train— the old wheel turned and turned anew, wearing my life away; but if it wasn't this wheel it would be another.

Rose, my stepmother, seemed glad to see me, smiling hard, speaking rapidly. 'We even thought you might come on the late train last night. We said he might be very well on that train when we heard it pass. We kept the kettle on till after the news, and then we said you'll hardly come now, but even then we didn't go to bed till we were certain you'd not come.'

'Is there something wrong?'

'No. There's nothing wrong.'

'What does he want me for?'

'I suppose he wants to see you. I didn't know there was anything special, but he's been worrying or brooding lately. I'm sure he'll tell you himself. And now you'll be wanting something to eat. He's not been himself lately,' she added conspiratorially. 'If you can, go with him, do your best to humour him.'

We shook hands when he came, but did not speak, and Rose and myself carried the burden of the conversation during the meal. Suddenly, as we rose at the end of the meal, he said, 'I want you to walk over with me and look at the walnuts.'

'Why the walnuts?'

'He's thinking of selling the walnut trees,' Rose said. 'They've offered a great price. It's for the veneer, but I said you wouldn't want us to sell.'

'A lot you'd know about that,' he said to her in a half-snarl, but she covertly winked at me, and we left it that way.

'Was the telegram about the selling of the walnut trees, then?' I asked as we walked together towards the plantation. 'Sell anything you want as far as I'm concerned.'

'No. I have no intention of selling the walnuts. I threaten to sell them from time to time, just to stir things up. She's fond of those damned walnuts. I just mentioned it as an excuse to get out. We can talk in peace here,' he said, and I waited.

'You know about this Act they're bringing in?' he began ponderously.

'No.'

'They're giving it a first reading, but it's not the law yet.'

'What is this Act?'

'It's an Act that makes sure that the widow gets so much of a man's property as makes no difference after he's dead—whether *he* likes it or not.'

'What's this got to do with us?'

'You can't be that thick. I'll not live for ever. After this Act who'll get this place? Now do you get my drift? Rose will. And who'll Rose give it to? Those damned relatives will be swarming all over this place before I'm even cold.'

'How do you know that?' I was asking questions now simply to gain time to think.

'How do I know?' he said with manic grievance. 'Already the place is disappearing fast beneath our feet. Only a few weeks back the tractor was missing. Her damned nephew had it. Without as much as by my leave. They forgot to inform me. And she never goes near them that there's not something missing from the house.'

'That's hardly fair. It's usual to share things round in the country. She always brought more back than she took.'

I remembered the baskets of raspberries and plums she used to bring back from their mountain farm.

'That's right. Don't take my word for it,' he shouted. 'Soon you'll know.'

'But what's this got to do with the telegram?' I asked, and he quietened.

'I was in to see Callan the solicitor. That's why I sent the telegram. If I transfer the place to you before that Act becomes law, then the Act can't touch us. Do you get me now?'

I did—too well. He would disinherit Rose by signing the place over to me. I would inherit both Rose and the place if he died.

'You won't have it signed over to you, then?'

'No, I won't. Have you said any of this to Rose?'

'Of course I haven't. Do you take me for a fool or some-thing? Are you saying to me for the last time that you won't take it?' And when I wouldn't answer he said with great bitterness, 'I should have known. You don't even have respect for your own blood,' and muttering, walked away towards the cattle gathered between the stone wall and the first of the walnut trees. Once or twice he moved as if he might turn back, but he did not. We did not speak any common language.

We avoided each other that evening, the tension making us prisoners of every small movement, and the next day I tried to slip away quietly.

'Is it going you are?' Rose said sharply when she saw me about to leave.

'That's right, Rose.'

'You shouldn't pass any heed on your father. You should let it go with him. He won't change his ways now. You're worse than he is, not to let it go with him.'

For a moment I wanted to ask her, 'Do you know that he wanted to leave you at my sweet mercy after his death?' but I knew she would answer, 'What does that matter? You know he gets these ideas. You should let it go with him;' and when I said, 'Goodbye, Rose,' she did not answer.

As the train trundled across the bridges into Dublin and by the grey back of Croke Park, all I could do was stare. The weekend was over like a life. If it had happened differently it would still be over. Differently, we would have had our walks and drinks, made love in the curtained rooms, experimented in the ways of love, pretending we were taming instinct, imagining we were getting more out of it than had been intended, and afterwards ... Where were we to go from there, our pleasure now its grinning head? And it would be over and not over. I had gone home instead, a grotesquerie of other homegoings, and it too was over now.

She would have met him at the airport, they would have had dinner, and if their evenings remained the same as when I used to meet them together they would now be having drinks in some bar. As the train came slowly into Amiens Street, I suddenly wanted to find them, to see us all together. They were not in any of the Grafton Street bars, and I was on the point of giving up the impulse— with gratitude that I hadn't been able to satisfy it—when I found them in a hotel lounge by the river. They were sitting at the corner, picking at a bowl of salted peanuts between their drinks. He seemed glad to see me, getting off his stool, 'I was just saying here how long it is since we last saw you,' in his remorseless slow voice, as if my coming might lighten an already heavy-hanging evening. He was so friendly that I could easily have asked him how his interview had gone, amid the profusion of my lies, forgetting that I wasn't supposed to know.

'I've just come from London. We've had dinner at the airport.' He began to tell me all that I already knew.

'And will you take this job?' I asked after he had told me at length about the weekend, without any attempt to select between details, other than to put the whole lot in.

'It's all arranged. It'll be in the papers tomorrow. I leave in three weeks' time,' he said.

'Congratulations,' I proffered uneasily. 'But do you have any regrets about leaving?'

'No. None whatever. I've done my marching stint and speeching stint. Let the young do that now. It's my time to sit back. There comes a time of life when your grapefruit in the morning is important.'

'And will your ladyship go with you?'

'I'll see how the land lies first, and then she'll follow. And by the way,' he began to shake with laughter and gripped my arm so that it hurt, 'don't you think to get up to anything with her while I'm gone.'

'Now that you've put it into my head I might try my hand.' I looked for danger but he was only enjoying his own joke, shaking with laughter as he rose from the bar stool. 'I better spend a penny on the strength of that.'

'That—was—mean,' she said without looking up.

'I suppose it was. I couldn't help it.'

'You knew we'd be around.'

'Will you see me tomorrow?'

'What do you think?'

'Anyhow, I'll be there.'

'How did your weekend in the country go?' she asked sarcastically.

'It went as usual, nothing but the usual,' I echoed her own sarcasm.

McCredy was still laughing when he came back. 'I've just been thinking that you two should be the young couple and me the uncle, and if you do decide to get up to something you must ask Uncle's dispensation first,' and he clapped me on the back.

'Well, I better start by asking now,' I said quickly in case my dismay would show, and he let out a bellow of helpless laughter. He must have been drinking, for he put his arms round both of us, 'I just love you two young people,' and tears of laughter slipped from his eyes. 'Hi, barman, give us another round before I die.'

I sat inside the partition in Gaffneys the next evening as on all other evenings, the barman as usual polishing glasses, nobody but the two of us in the bar.

'Your friend seems a bit later than usual this evening,' he said.

'I don't think she'll come this evening,' I said, and he looked at me inquiringly. 'She went down the country for the weekend. She was doubtful if she'd get back.'

'I hope there's nothing wrong ...'

'No. Her mother is old. You know the way.' I was making for the safety of the roomy clichés.

'That's the sadness. You don't know whether to look after them or your own life.'

Before any pain of her absence could begin to hang about the opening and closing doors as the early evening drinkers bustled in, I got up and left; and yet her absence was certainly less painful than the responsibility of a life together. But what then of love? Love flies out the window, I had heard them say.

'She'll not come now,' I said.

'No. It doesn't seem,' he said as he took my glass with a glance in which suspicion equalled exasperation.

We did not meet till several weeks later. We met in Grafton Street, close to where we had met the first night. A little nervously she agreed to come for a drink with me. She looked quite beautiful, a collar of dark fur pinned to her raincoat.

'Jerry's in Sierra Leone now,' she said when I brought the drinks.

'I know. I read it in the papers.'

'He rang me last night,' she said. 'He was in the house of a friend—a judge. I could hear music in the background. I think they were a bit tight. The judge insisted he speak to me too. He had an Oxford accent. Very posh but apparently he's as black as the ace of spades,' she laughed. I could see that she treasured the wasteful call more than if it had been a gift of brilliant stones.

She began to tell me about Sierra Leone, its swamps and markets, the avocado and pineapple and cacao and banana trees, its crocodile-infested rivers. Jerry lived in a white-columned house with pillars on a hillside above the sea, and he had been given a chauffeur-driven Mercedes. She laughed when she told me that a native bride had to spend the first nine months of her marriage indoors so that she grew light-skinned.

'Will you be joining Jerry soon?' I asked.

'Soon. He knows enough people high up now to arrange it. They're getting the papers in order.'

'I don't suppose you'll come home with me tonight, then?'

'No.' There wasn't a hint of hesitation in the answer; difficulty and distance were obviously great restorers of the moral order. 'You must let me take you to dinner, then, before you leave. As old friends. No strings attached,' I smoothed.

'That'll be nice,' she said.

Out in Grafton Street we parted as easily as two leaves sent spinning apart by any sudden gust. All things begin in dreams, and it must be wonderful to have your mind full of a whole country like Sierra Leone before you go there and risk discovering that it might be your life.

Nothing seems ever to end except ourselves. On the eve of her departure for Sierra Leone, another telegram came from the country. There was nothing mysterious about it this time. Rose had died.

The overnight bag, the ticket, the train ...

The iron gate under the yew was open and the blinds of the stone house at the end of the gravel were drawn. Her flower garden, inside the wooden gate in the low whitethorn hedge just before the house, had been freshly weeded and the coarse grass had been cut with shears. Who would tend the flowers now? I shook hands with everybody in the still house, including my father, who did not rise from the converted car chair.

I heard them go over and over what happened, as if by going over and over it they would return it to the every-day. 'Rose got up, put on the fire, left the breakfast ready, and went to let out the chickens. She had her hand on the latch coming in, when he heard this thump, and there she was lying, the door half-open.' And they were succeeding. They had to. She had too much of the day.

I went into the room to look on her face. The face was over too. If she had been happy or unhappy it did not show now. Would she have been happier with another? Who knows the person another will find their happiness or unhappiness with? Enough to say that weighed in this scale it makes little difference or every difference.

'Why don't you let it go with him?' I heard her voice. 'You know what he's like.' She had lived rooted in this one place and life, with this one man, like the black sally in the one hedge, as pliant as it is knobbed and gnarled, keeping close to the ground as it invades the darker corners of the meadows.

The coffin was taken in. The house was closed. I saw some of the mourners trample on the flowers as they waited in the front garden for her to be taken out. She was light on our shoulders.

Her people did not return to the house after the funeral. They had relinquished any hopes they had to the land.

'We seem to have it all to ourselves,' I said to my father in the empty house. He gave me a venomous look but did not reply for long.

'Yes,' he said. 'Yes. We seem to have it all to ourselves. But where do we go from here?'

Not, anyhow, to Sierra Leone. For a moment I saw the tall colonial building on a hill above the sea, its white pillars, the cool of the veranda in the evening ... Maybe they were facing one another across a dinner table at this very moment, a servant removing the dishes.

Where now is Rose?

I see her come on a bicycle, a cane basket on the handlebars. The brakes mustn't be working for she has to jump off and run alongside the bicycle. Her face glows with happiness as she pulls away the newspaper that covers the basket. It is full of dark plums, and eggs wrapped in pieces of newspaper are packed here and there among the plums. Behind her there shivers an enormous breath of pure sky.

'Yes,' my father shouted. 'Where do we go from here?'

'I suppose we might as well try and stay put for a time,' I answered, and when he looked at me sharply I added, for the sake of my own peace, 'that is, until things settle a bit, and we can find our feet again, and think.'

Four Green Fields

Val Mulkerns

The house seemed empty when they got in from the road, but Denis made a quick tour of the upstairs rooms just in case his wife might be getting ready to go out. The American girl, in pink and white gingham, tagged along behind.

'Sometimes I dream of this house,' she said. 'And then I smell apples and hear the pigeons make their clamour in that tree out there. Like the first time I came. Like every time.'

'Not this pigeon,' Denis said. He stood transfixed in the door of the room with a sudden feeling of horror he couldn't explain. His guest stood behind him as though in a bus queue. On the bed near the open window was a young pinkish bird with folded wings and head buried in the tufted white cotton of the bedspread. It lay as though floating head downwards on water.

'Asleep,' Mary Kate said, amazed, following him across the room. 'Asleep like a person on a bed.'

'Dead like a person on a bed,' Denis corrected. There was no blood anywhere, not even when the girl lifted up the plump warm body in her hands. But on the mantelpiece among the blue glass floats and chunks of rock and photograph of Sarah at school there were a few feathers slightly bloodstained at the tips. The blood was already dry. Man and girl walked from the mantelpiece to the open window and back again to the warm hollow on the fluffy cotton where the bird had lain.

'A hawk?' Mary Kate guessed.

'In inner suburbia? I hardly think so. But I think this was an inexpert flyer who misjudged the open window. He probably hit the mantelpiece with some force and all the damage happened under the feathers. He was half stunned, and could fly no further than the bed.'

'So he died tidily on it,' the girl said. 'So goddamn tidily.' Rocking the body of the pigeon in her arms she began to laugh wildly so that her companion couldn't be sure at what point the laughter dissolved. 'Last year they pumped me for three hours in hospital when all I wanted was to die tidily like this one.'

'That was last year,' Denis said firmly, taking the dead bird from her with hands that were still shaking. 'You are a year older and much more sensible and your good thesis on John Millington Synge is entirely prepared and already half written. You're going to be all *right*. Come downstairs and I'll make you some coffee. Come on.' But first he remembered to pick the few feathers off the carpet where they had drifted, and he remembered to search till he found a single dried spot of blood on the white mantelpiece which he wiped away. He didn't want to trouble Emily with any traces.

In the kitchen was the old cat, eager for company, and a note from Emily. Mary Kate read it aloud as her host disposed of the dead bird in the incinerator.

> 'Think I'll go straight on from town to O'Sullivan's where they plan to eat early (seven-thirty for eight o'clock, remember?). Will you follow on when you get back—they'll be disappointed if you miss it. Love. E.
>
> 'PS Hope Mary Kate met her father all right and that you aren't too tired after the long drive back. Liver for the cat in the fridge – can you believe it? E.'

'What will she say Denis? I can't just *be* here when you both get back.'

'You'll come with me to the party, that's what you'll do. I'll phone to fix it with Siobhán O'Sullivan. It's an open sort of house anyway. We haven't seen them since we got back from holidays so it's certain to be a cheerful evening.'

'But what will Emily *say* when she hears I ran away from my father and back to here again?'

'She'll most likely tell you Sarah's room is free and you can stay here till you decide when you do want to go to the west.'

'But Denis, do *you* even understand? I couldn't go up to him at Shannon because I saw whiskey in his hand and when he drinks—which he probably did because he had to face seeing me after two years and a new wife I've never seen—he goes on and on and on and it can last for weeks ...'

'Stop thinking about it now. I'll make your coffee after I've fed the cat. Why don't you go out and air yourself in the garden? Emily has a seat in the sun out there—look.'

As he stooped to pick up his ragged cat, the girl stooped too and kissed the back of his neck. 'Run out like a good child and I'll bring you coffee out there,' Denis said smoothly, and because her gesture had been totally ignored the girl obeyed, shaking her head baffled as she went. The clock up in the hall struck the hour. Half past five. The garden was loud with birdsong.

Town was sultry and grey and Emily had a message to do for an elderly relative which took her all over the city and finally to a part of it she seldom saw these days. Talbot Street used to be 'town' when she was a child, always crammed on Friday with large female shoppers who butted children in the face with full shopping bags and never apologized. The way to pass relatively unharmed was to hold your head up and keep your eyes fixed on Nelson on top of his pillar. That way you might sustain bruised elbows or sore ribs but your face had a chance of remaining undamaged. That way also you had a chance of losing your mother which was a terrifying thing when it happened. What you did then was stay exactly where you were until she found you. That was the rule. You didn't look for her or you were lost indeed. Emily had a vague memory of such an occasion and of subsequent comforting in Bewley's on the other side of O'Connell Bridge but visits to Bewley's were expensive and mainly connected with Christmas or the annual pilgrimage to buy school shoes in Bradley's.

Talbot Street was now both brighter and shabbier than it used to be, full of boutiques blaring pop music and selling trendy gear of American origin, T-shirts stamped with declarations of one sort or another, denim garments of every kind including underwear. Older establishments selling furniture or books or matrons' drapery had grown dimmer and shabbier, brick fronts no longer cleaned or pointed, awaiting the moment when the owners would sell out and the shopfront be adorned with yet another paper banner announcing another boutique or another cheap Indian bazaar. The general seediness reminded her of the one place in the known world she found dismaying, Praed Street in London, where faint painted medallions on the crumbling brick proclaimed 'Surgical and sexual appliances a speciality'.

She doubted if even in Praed Street the piece of apparel formerly known as a 'modesty vest' could be found. The elderly relative had been specific however about the places in Dublin likely to stock this garment of her youth but she had been proved wrong. Merry's of Talbot Street had been suggested by a friend of Emily's. Crossing the street to the shop at the traffic lights, she was beside a young family setting out apparently for a late afternoon stroll in Stephen's Green. A flaxen-haired toddler carried in one hand a crumpled brown paper bag whose contents Emily could guess. The other hand was held by the child's father who looked as if he ought to be still at school. The ducks, he was saying, might be well fed by now since it was getting a bit late in the day, but the seagulls were greedy buggers and could always put away more grub. The child said she didn't want to feed the seagulls. Her equally young mother pushed a go-car with a smaller child fallen asleep sideways on a pink pillow. Just before they reached the pavement where there was a parked car, the long-haired girl glanced back to check that her family hadn't been cut off by a change of lights, and then quite suddenly the world exploded all around them in flames and noise and falling mortar. Emily seemed to be looking down from a great height through clouds of smoke at bodies with open mouths from which no sound came.

This story, like two or three very similar ones, would last Feardorcha O'Briain all night. He was a senior counsel who took mostly Provo briefs these days. His story would be abandoned several times in the course of the meal and taken up again if a gap presented itself in the conversation. It was long and dull and concerned details of the Coventry bombing in 1940. Very often it sidetracked back to 1916. Sometimes he interrupted the story himself with verses from a newish ballad of which he approved. He had the remains of a good parlour voice.

> '"What did I have?" said the fine old woman,
> "What did I have?" this fine old woman would say,
> "I had four green fields and each one was a jewel
> But strangers came and tried to take them from me."'

A young American couple researching a book on the influence of revolutionary history on Anglo-Irish literature had heard most of the Coventry story before and tomorrow after breakfast in Percy Place they would go over their notes yet again with a bright red marker indicating cross references.

'Siobhán, a chroí,[1] won't you send Emily over to me as soon as she arrives, till I see would she remember whether it was the Da or Jimmy Mallon took the rise out of the camp commander that time on armistice night? Virginia here is very particular about the details, aren't you, my treasure?'

Virginia O'Hagan was adept at avoiding the large encircling hand but smiled pacifically at him and nodded her head. She had already noted the bottle of whiskey stashed away against the wall. These times he didn't travel without adequate personal supplies, she had been told.

'Yes, a tincture if you please, Brian, and would you switch on the news till we see what way the world is at all at all?'

'Siobhán wants us to sit down and eat very soon—is it worthwhile?'

'You'd never know, you'd never know what you might miss, maybe a particularly important commercial,' O'Briain said.

'Well anyhow Denis and Emily haven't got here yet,' the host agreed, switching on the television set. A panel game

---

[1] Irish term of endearment, meaning 'my heart'.

was nearing its end but after a couple of seconds there was a news flash.

> Details are becoming clearer about this afternoon's car bomb explosion in Dublin's Talbot Street. It has been established that at least twenty people have been killed outright and dozens injured, some of them seriously. Emergency services are in operation. A full report will follow the Nuacht[2] at eight o'clock.

Outside in the hall the phone was ringing above the shocked clamour of the guests and Brian went to answer it. 'Yes, yes of course. Bring her and welcome—no problem. Have you heard the shocking news?'

He gave it briefly and noted the long gasp from Denis at the other end before he asked whether Emily had arrived yet. She was to have come straight on from town. 'No, Denis, she's not here yet, but it's much too early to get worried. Town must be in chaos because of the bombing—you can imagine the traffic jams. Come over at once and we'll all worry together.'

The host dodged briefly back into the kitchen to tell his wife Siobhán, who covered her eyes in horror and began to gibber about Emily. She most probably had been in Talbot Street that afternoon because Siobhán herself had suggested Merry's as a possible place to find some

---

[2] The Irish-language news programme on the main television station.

outmoded garment for the old aunt. And then suddenly the doorbell rang and there was Emily in the porch, white-faced, bloodstained, filthy, but unquestionably alive and begging a pound to pay for her taxi. It was unlikely, Emily said, she'd ever see her handbag again. And then almost immediately her husband was rushing up the path to clasp her in disbelief.

'No panic,' he said. 'I've paid off your man. O, Emily.'

They were laughing then and embracing like lovers. Emily was apologizing for not phoning at once—there were queues a mile long at all the phone boxes. Into the hall edged the girl in pink gingham to join the groups of friends waiting until their presence was noticed. The girl's presence had however been noted by Emily in a quick exasperated smile.

'Tell you the story later, Emily,' her husband said in her ear. 'She ran like a redshank from her father so I suppose we'll have to put her up for a few days.'

'Fine, she can have Sarah's room,' Emily said.

'I lapped up superstition with my mother's milk, did you know that?' Denis was saying. 'And I haven't drawn an easy breath since I found a dead pigeon on our bed this afternoon.'

'How apposite the knave was,' Emily quipped. 'A witty bird, if dead itself.'

'You're not dead anyhow.' He hugged her again and they turned to face the impatient people in the hall, both of them embarrassed by their self-absorption.

'I'm sorry to be late and glad to be alive.' Emily smiled, and then the questions rained on her. 'No, no, I was thrown clear,' she said. 'All I have is a bruised elbow where I was flung against a hotel railings. Look, that's all. But the first three people I tried to help turned out not to need it—not ever again. And two babies on their way to feed the ducks in Stephen's Green, as Sarah used to do, were blown into fragments. One moment the one who could walk was talking to her father and carrying her paper bag of bread, and the next moment she wasn't there any more and I never saw her again. But I saw them carrying her father away on a stretcher with something clutched tight in his hand—the baby's hand, I think. I saw so many people being gathered into plastic bags.'

Emily began to shiver violently and was taken away to a warm bath by her hosts. When she appeared half an hour later she was calm and clean with wet hair, arrayed in one of Siobhán's long cottons which was too big for her. Fear-dorcha O'Briain made a cavalier bow to her, removed his tie and offered it to her as a belt. The Americans noted that he must have been handsome once and very like Michael Collins. Emily fastened the tie on and they all sat down. O'Briain was unsteady but didn't seem drunker than usual.

The host thought their food would be attacked with raging appetites but nobody except O'Briain ate much. It wasn't until the coffee stage had been reached that they realized just how drunk he was. Almost a full bottle of wine had been added to his day's quota and now when the host unwisely passed around the brandy, O'Briain poured it for himself as though it were wine. He had been making no more of a nuisance of himself to his immediate neighbours than usual until somebody mentioned the bombing again and then he staggered to his feet as though addressing a public meeting, raised his glass and shouted: 'I give you the beginning of the end, friends. Every bomb that shatters capitalist complacency in the south brings us nearer to the day when there will be a final withdrawal of enemy troops from Ireland. When that day dawns north and south will be united in bloodshed—Christ knows nothing was ever achieved without bloodshed in the history of this unfortunate island. After Ireland's second civil war there will be an end to the effects of seven hundred years of foreign domination. We have to bring the fight down here into the south by any and every means in our power because there is no other way to the ultimate aim of a United Irish Socialist Republic.'

'Is bombing babies in prams north and south a permissible means to this end?' That was Emily, white-faced again.

'Regrettable but inevitable, my treasure.' The eyes were mad and bloodshot now but his articulation was professionally perfect. 'You won't have forgotten that a prematurely senile politician said six years ago that we wouldn't stand idly by and watch our people in the north tortured and beaten back into the ground by the forces of imperialism? But by the sweet suffering Jesus we did stand idly by and we'll go on doing it whatever fucking lot of power-drunk gombeen men are in power in Dáil Éireann until we are made to see that the crisis is not the north's problem but ours, the concern of all of us, and that the only way forward is total reshaping of our society after a civil war that is, any way, inevitable. It's not and it never was "a little local difficulty" as that imbecile Eden said about Suez. It's the finish of the job that was begun in blood at Easter sixty years ago, and won't end until the Brits get out and the streets of every town in the south run redder with blood than the streets of Belfast will tonight.'

Unstoppable now, he rebounded suddenly on the Americans. 'What we want from you, friends, is money and guns, not theses. Fuck the half-baked phoney talk of John Millington Synge that obsesses you and his sorry dozens of imitators. The landowning classes like your William

Butler Yeats and George Moore and Augusta Gregory made a career for themselves out of the craven quaintness of a poverty-stricken tenantry. We want no more patronizing Anglo-Irish geniuses and no more quaint peasants or urban slaves. I regret as much as the next man the death of children and civilians that is a necessary adjunct of the urban guerrilla warfare all over the world. We have to end suffering by temporarily making more of it—we have to ...'

The big drunken historic ruin of a man stopped abruptly as the American couple with a gentle touch on the shoulders of their hosts left the room. Emily followed, glad that somebody had taken the initiative, and somebody else at the table poured more coffee for O'Briain and pulled him back into his chair. He deliberately took up the cup and poured it over the tablecloth before staggering to his feet and up the stairs. The host followed with Denis, who offered to drive O'Briain home. Nobody would be sorrier or quicker to phone with his apologies in the morning than the same parlatic madman, Denis said.

In the next room Emily switched on the television for the late news, and the little huddle of people around her heard more reports of deaths in the city casualty wards. Also two Catholics had been shot dead in a village pub in Armagh and four Protestants seriously injured when masked raiders sprayed a Sandy Row lounge with machine-gun fire. A member of the Westminster opposition had been slightly injured in a car bomb explosion outside his Mayfair flat, and news had just come through of the death in mysterious circumstances of an Irish student in Paris.

Meanwhile outside in the hall were the sounds of O'Briain's departure. His hosts held him upright while Denis brought around the car and he continued in a maudlin bellow to lament the fourth green field of the proud old woman whose sons had sons brave as were their fathers. Emily sat listening among the friends who remained.

'When I was ten,' she said, shivering, 'I had that man's picture pinned up on my wall at home. With Pearse and Dev and Yeats and Bold Robert Emmet.'

I nGleic ('In a Pickle')

Dara Ó Conaola

Dónall Ó Conaill a tharraing an mí-adh is mó orm—tar éis chomh molta is a bhíodh sé ag Clanna Gael; deamhan aithne orthu nach é Dia acu é. Is fíor go mbíodh sé molta agam féin, freisin. Dhéanfainn a raibh i mo chumas lena onóir a chosaint, lá ar bith. Dhéanfainn lá saoire dó. Dhéanfainn sin go cinnte—go dtí an oíche sin.

* * * * *

'Cén áit é siúd a raibh mé?'

'Sa mBaile Mór seo, ar ndóigh, a bhí tú.'

'Tá a fhios agam go rí-mhaith gurbh ea—ach cén áit ann?'

'Bhí tú sa bpub údan a mbítheá i gcónaí ann. Nár chaith tú tráthnóna fada ann.'

'Cá ndeachaigh mé ansin?'

'Dúirt tú ar deireadh go raibh tú ag dul ag imeacht. Ní choinneodh tada thú. D'imigh tú. Ní cuimhin liom tada eile faoi sin ...'

* * * * *

Caithfidh sé, tharla nach féidir linn cuimhniú air, nach mbeidh muid in ann a dhéanamh amach go deo go beacht cá ndeachaigh mé ansin. Ach, tá mé cinnte dearfa go ndeachaigh mé cúpla áit le linn an ama atá faoi thrácht. Caithfidh sé gur chaith mé an t-am in áit éigin, mar níor chuala mé riamh gur éalaigh aon chúpla uair an chloig amach as an saol gan é a chaitheamh in áit éigin, ar chuma éigin ...

Thart anuas le Coláiste na Tríonóide, is dócha, a tháinig mé. Síos liom ansin go dtí an droichead scóipiúil a dtugann siad Droichead Uí Chonaill air. Droichead Dhónaillín na Gaeilge, ainmnithe i ndiaidh an Ghaeil-geora is cáiliúla dár mhair ariamh. Nach í an Ghaeilge a shábháil é babhta nuair a bhí sé i gcruachás, lá dá chuid laethanta móra anallód. Tá a fhios ag an saol é.

'A Dhónaill Uí Chonaill, an dtuigeann tú Gaeilge', a dúirt an cailín ó Éirinn leis agus í ag freastal ar bhord mór galánta thall i Londain.

'Céard sin is léir duit', a dúirt mo Dhónall, gan chuimhne ar thada aige—ach an oiread is a bhí agam féin an oíche sin.

'Á', a deir sí, 'bíodh a fhios agat go bhfuil nimh i do chupán a mharódh na céadta!'

Níor thuig aon duine eile a bhí i láthair an chaint. Ach bhí Ó Conaill san airdeall. D'fhreagair sé i mBéarla:

'Ar mhiste leat gloine fíoruisce a thabhairt chugam ina áit?'

Tháinig sé slán ón gcontúirt.

Is fada an lá anois ó d'airigh mé an scéal sin ag Seáinín Dorcha.

''Sí, mais', a deir Seáinín, 'an Ghaeilge a shábháil é ...'

Go ndéana Dia grásta ar Sheáinín Dorcha, is ar Dhónall, is ar an gcailín ó Éirinn—is orm féin ...

Is cuimhin liom an Droichead. Ní cuimhin liom duine ná deoraí, carr ná bus, ná rud ar bith eile a fheiceáil ag gluaiseacht ann, ach an droichead ciúin folamh. Soilse sráide ag lonrú go healaíonta.

Dónall féin, ar ndóigh, bhí sé ann. Agus a chuid aingle.

Labhair mé leis go lách laethúil, mar is dual dom. Caithfidh sé gur i nGaeilge nó i mBéarla a labhair mé—mar níl Laidin ná Fraincis ná Gréigis ná teanga na bhfaoileán ar eolas agam ró-mhaith.

Pé ar bith teanga a labhair mé níor thug sé aon aird orm.

Déarfaidh mé an fhírinne ghlan, níl rud ar bith sa saol is mó a chuireann olc ormsa ná an chluais bhodhar bhalbh ghránna seo ó aon duine—ó aon neach. Is cuma cé í féin nó céard é féin.

Bhí a fhios agam go maith gur bheag caint a d'fhéadfadh fear cloiche mar é a dhéanamh. Ach d'fhéadfadh sé ligean air féin. Is iomaí caoi le rud a dhéanamh nuair a thagann an tairne ar an troigh. D'fhéadfadh sé é a chur in iúl dom istigh i mo chroí go deas discréideach, mar tá mo chroí i gcónaí oscailte le glacadh le teachtaireachtaí taitneamhacha ... Gur airigh sé céard a dúirt mé, go raibh sé buíoch díom, a bheith ag dul abhaile anois, chuig do bhean is do chuid gasúr, má tá a leithéidí agat ... nó más mac léinn thú, téigh ar ais chuig t'árasán agus chuig do chuid leabhra scoile ... agus fág mise mar atá mé ar mo ardán uasal. Sin é a déarfadh sé dá mbeadh cuma air. Ach mo léan! An siolla fhéin níor chuala mé in aon teanga uaidh, rud a ghoill orm—go mór.

Mar sin féin, de bhrí gur gheall Dia foighid dom, agus ós rud é gur éirigh liom cuimhniú ar chúpla seanfhocal a dtabharfainn aird orthu, dúirt mé liom féin go dtabharfainn seans eile dó.

'Go mbeannaí Dia agus Muire dhuit, a Dhónaill Uí Chonaill,' a dúirt mé, 'an tráth álainn seo dhár saol.'

I nGaeilge bhlasta mhilis na nGael a labhair mé agus, ní as ucht mé féin á rá é, chomh líofa céanna is a déarfadh mo sheanmhuintir é, agus deirtear gur fearr i bhfad an Ghaeilge a labhraítí an t-am sin ná anois. Ach ba bheag an mhaith dhom sin. Tháinig mé ar an tuiscint dá mba í Gaeilge Bhriain Bóraimhe a bheadh agam nach

dtabharfadh Dónall uaibhreach aon toradh orm. An clad-
haire ceanndána.

Faoi seo, bhí an lasóg sa bharrach eadrainn. An meas a
bhíodh agam air, bhí sé anois ag iompó go tapa ina fhearg,
cuthach feirge. Bhí spéir chiúin na hoíche ag cuir strainc
an oilc uirthi féin.

'Maise, nár fheice Dia an t-ádh go brách ort', a dúirt mé
leis go feargach. Bhí rún agam píosa maith den teanga a
thabhairt dó, a bhainfeadh cuid den éirí in airde de … ag
déanamh rí dhe fhéin thuas ansin chomh postúil agus a
cheann go hard sa spéirsholas cathrach aige.

Déarfainn suas lena bhéal é.

Thug mé aghaidh air, cé gur dhána an mhaise dhom
é. Is dócha, an té a d'fheicfeadh mé, go raibh cuma
dhrochmhúinte, thaodach orm, nó lena chur i dtéarmaí
státseirbhíse—mí-rialta.

Ach is gearr gur raibh dream an-rialta ar fad i mo thim-
peall, iad ag déanamh orm ó gach aon taobh. Staiceanna
diongbháilte na lámh láidir a bhí ann. Trioblóid.

Tharraing mé mo chlaíomh ceann airgid ar luas lasrach.

'Caith uait an claíomh in ainm an dlí', a d'fhógair fear
acu orm go húdarásach.

'Fanaigí fad buille uaim,' a dúirt mise, chomh
húdarásach céanna, beagnach, ar ais leis.

'Tá an dlí briste agat,' a dúirt sé, 'agus caithfidh muid tú a
thógáil. Tusa!', a dúirt sé, 'níl aon dliteanas agatsa sa gcás.'

'Tusa!' a dúirt mise leis, 'níl an dliteanas ceart agat. Tá claíomh agamsa. Tá mé in ann troid.'

'Beidh a fhios againn faoi sin gan mórán moille.'

'Beidh a fhios,' a dúirt mise, 'agus rud eile dhe, tá dhá thaobh ar an achrann seo.'

'Céard sa deabhal atá tú a'rá? Tá muide anseo le thú a ghabháil. Níl an dara leagan ar an scéal. Ná bí ag cur ár gcuid ama amú.'

'Tá an choimhlint seo idir beirt. Má tá tú ag iarraidh am a shábháil, tógfaidh sibh an fear eile freisin,'ag díriú a n-airde ar Ó Conaill.' Sin é an t-aon chaoi a mbeidh mise sásta a theacht libh go síochánta.'

Thost sé agus bhreathnaigh sé timpeall ar na fir eile. Rinne siad comhrá beag i dteanga aisteach gan aon chaint. Níor thuig mé oiread is focal amháin den chogarnach aisteach sin.'

'Foighid ort nóiméad,'a dúirt sé, de ghlór níos ciúine, níos cairdiúla, cheap mé. 'Tógfaidh muid Ó Conaill freisin, má chaitheann tú uait an, um, claíomh agus teacht linn go síochánta. Is muide an dlí. Gheobhaidh tú aire mhaith. Céard a déarfá leis sin?'

'Ach, an féidir liom sibh a thrust?'

'Cinnte glan, is féidir. Ar son na síochána a bhíonn muide, cloíonn muid go dlúth leis an gcóras. Chomh maith leis sin, go pearsanta tugaim m'fhocal dhuit air. Céard faoi sin?'

'An bhfuil tú sásta mionnú os comhair a bhfuil anseo anois agus os comhair na n-aingeal?'

Chrom sé a chloigeann go dearfa, an chaoi ar roghnaigh sé le 'táim' a rá.

Chuaigh sé síos ar a leathghlúin agus mhionnaigh sé dhom agus do chuile dhuine eile, go seasfadh sé lena fhocal. Ar an gcúis sin, chaith mé uaim an claíomh álainn a bhuaigh mé cúpla bliain ó shoin nuair a fuair mé an chéad duais i gcomórtas damhsa ar an sean-nós ag an bhFleá Cheoil.

* * * * *

Ar an bpointe a tharla an méid sin, tharla rud eile— nár thaitin liom, beag ná mór.

Thosaigh an ciorcal de na fir mhóra na lámh láidir ag cúngú isteach orm, Léimeadar orm. Rugadar abhus is thall orm. Rug duine acu ar chluais orm. Cuireadh fuinneamh i mo láimh.

Caitheadh isteach sa charr mór dubh, a dtugann daoine Máire Dhubh air, mé. Bhí mé sáinnithe.

As go brách le Máire Dhubh. D'fhágadar Ó Conaill mar a bhí sé! Go buacach stáidiúil.

Níor thaitin an éagóir seo liom, tar éis ar ghealladar, ar mhionnaíodar. Bhí cuthach dearg orm. Bhí feall déanta orm. Á! bhí mé ar buille.

'Is cam an dlí atá agaibh,' a dúirt mé.

Níor dúradh tada.

'Ach níl sé chomh cam libh féin, a phaca deabhal. Tá sibh chomh cam le cos deiridh gadhair, chomh dúr le slis.'

Buille sna heasnacha, agus múr mionnaí móra mar anlann leis, an freagra a tugadh air sin.

Chuir mise mionnaí móra ina ndiaidh féin, ag athrá na gcinn a caitheadh liom.

Chuireadar ar mo shúile dom, go pras go mbeadh cúis i m'aghaidh faoi a bheith ag mallachtú.

'Más ea,' a dúirt mise, 'tá sé chomh maith domh an chúis a shaothrú go maith.'

Gach uile dhrochfhocal dár chuala mé riamh, ó d'fhág mé an baile go dtí sin, scaoil mé amach iad ina liodán— agus fuair mé 'guí orainn' deas sna heasnacha i ndiaidh gach uile cheann. Chuir cuid de na focail níos mó oilc orthu ná a chéile. Thug mé 'bobarún' ar dhuine dhíobh agus chuir sé an-olc air. 'Gurrier', sin ceann eile nár thaitin leo ar chor ar bith. Ach an ceann is mó a chuir le buile iad ná 'Dúchrónach.' Mar sin, choinnigh mé orm á rá sin aríst agus aríst eile, leis an am a mheilt. Ní raibh mórán ama ar chor ar bith meilte nó go raibh muid ag an 'stáisiún', mar a thug said air. Beairic a thugaimse air.

Faoi seo, bhí mé ag éirí tuirseach go leor, cheal bídh— agus dí.

Is cuimhin liom an Bheairic go maith. Tharraing siad isteach go dtí seomra cúil mé. Bhí cathaoir ag fanacht liom.

Tháinig glór údarásach amach as ceithre chúinne na síleála, ar aon ghuth: 'Bí i do shuí!'

Ghlac me leis an ordú.

Bhí beirt ar m'aghaidh agus duine ar mo chúl. Thosaigh an ceistiú.

'T'ainm? An bhfuil tú in ann a dhearbhú gur Seán, sin é an t-ainm a fuair muid ó do pháirtí óil, an fear a dtugtar "An Cop" air—ní gan fáth,' agus é ag díriú a airde ar an bhfear ar mo chúl. 'A bé sin t-ainm?'

Lig mé bodhaire Uí Laoire orm fhéin.

'Cé tú féin ... Céard atá i do phócaí?'

Bodhaire Uí Laoire.

'An bhfuil tú i do bhall d'eagras mídhleathach?'

Balbh.

Ba mise an máistir anois, a cheap mé, agus ba mé nó go mbainfidís eolas asam—rud nach raibh aon rún agamsa a thabhairt dóibh. Thug an smaoineamh seo beagán uchtaigh dom.

'Dhá mbeadh coir féin déanta agam ní bhfaigheadh sibh amach go deo é leis na ceisteanna leibideacha atá sibh a chur, a phleidhcí amadáin, a ...'

'Cé air a bhfuil tú ag tabhairt "mada"?'

'Ní thabharfainn mada oraibhse,' a dúirt mé, 'is ainmhí uasal é an mada. Ní hionann is sibhse.'

Bhuail taghd duine acu agus thug sé buille ar an bpus dom, a d'airigh mé.

Chaith siad uair an chloig, beagnach, do mo phoicneáil, is do mo bhualadh, do mo cheistiú.

Ach níor inis mé tada dóibh.

* * * * *

Ar deireadh d'árdaigh siad síos go dtí cillín mé. Tugadh pluid dom agus fuair mé ordú a dhul a chodladh—rud a rinne mé go fonnmhar.

Ach ní raibh mé ach ar tí titim i mo chodladh ar an leaba dheas chrua adhmaid nuair a d'airigh mé ag déanamh orm arís iad. Ó a dheabhail, ní féidir!

Ó a dheabhail, is féidir. Duine nua a bhí ann. Fear meánaosta, é i bhfad níos sibhialta ná an chuid eile. É deas go leor liom freisin. Ach ní mheallfadh sé mise—chuimhnigh mé ar an gcleas a d'imir said orm cheana, gan Ó Conaill a thógáil mar a gheall siad.

Ach bhí a fhios agam freisin nach bhfaighinn aon suaimhneas uathu muna ndéanfainn méid áithrid éigin comhoibriú leo. Mar sin labhair mé leis an bhfear meánaosta:

'Ní inseoidh mé tada anocht', a dúirt mé leis,' ach má thógann sibh Ó Conaill, mar a gheall sibh, amárach nuair a ghabhfas mé i gcomhairle le dlíodóir, tabharfaidh mé an t-eolas uilig daoibh.'

'Um,' a dúirt sé.

Bhí mé ag súil gurbh ionann 'um' agus 'tá mé sásta leis an socrú sin.' Smaoinigh sé ar feadh nóiméid, sular labhair sé:

'Ceart go leor,' a dúirt sé.

D'éirigh sé ina sheasamh go tobann agus amach leis.

D'imigh leis, agus ní cuimhin liom tada eile faoi sin.

* * * * *

Tháinig an mhaidin le bánú an lae. An chúirt. Sin í a bhí romham ansin, an chloch ba mhó ar mo phaidrín. Shocraigh mé gurbh fhearr dhom a dhul leis an sruth, pé ar bith cá dtabharfadh an taoille mé. Ní raibh aon chúrsa eile fágtha agam le leanacht.

Bhí an mhaidin caite agam ag dul ó chillín go cillín. 'Ba mheasa an fanacht ná an chúirt.' Ab é go bhfuil mo shaol mar a bheadh seanfhocal seanchaite ann, faoin tráth seo!

Cuireadh isteach i gcillín i dTeach na Cúirte ar dtús mé. Beirt den lucht siúil a mbínn cairdiúil leo romham ann. Trí leaba adhmaid a bhí ann. Luigh mé ar cheann. D'oscail an doras mór. Tae a bhí ag teacht. Mo dhá chomrádaí ag éirí go tapa nuair a d'airigh siad an tae ag teacht.

Sáspainín tae agus sliseog de bhuilín á leagan in aice liomsa. É socraithe agamsa a dhul ar stailc ocrais ag an bpointe seo. Mise ag éirí de léim. Ag tabhairt mo sheanchic don tae.

Níor dhúirt an Garda bocht tada os ard, ach bhí mise ag éisteacht leis ag cuimhniú air féin: 'Coinneoidh mé e sin i gcuimhne ... le cur lena chuntas cúiseanna. Níl mise ach ag déanamh mo jab.' Bhí mé ag fáil níos eolaí ar a dteanga bhalbh rúnda faoi seo. Bhí gardaí na maidine níos deise ná dream na hoíche aréir, cheap mé.

Bhí mé ag fanacht. Agus, in am agus i dtráth, glaodh orm.

* * * * *

Tugadh síos go dtí íochtar Theach na Cúirte mé. Bhí halla fada ann. Ag ceann an halla bhí staighre cloch agus dúirt an garda liom seasamh ansin agus fanacht le treoracha breise; rud a rinne muid ar feadh nóiméid, nó dhó, sílim ...

'Suas leat anois', a deir an Garda liom.

Suas liom, linn.

Isteach liom sa chúirt. Seoladh mé go dtí m'áit chuí. Bhí an Giúistís amach romham agus Cléireach lena thaobh. Cléireach eile an taobh eile. Cléireachaí eile Stáit ina suí leis an mballa ar chaon taobh de sheomra na cúirte. Bhí baicle eile, fir agus mná dea-ghléasta ina seasamh ar mo chúl. Lucht éisteachta, cheap mé.

'Seo é an duine gan ainm', a dúirt an Giúistís

'Is é, a Ghiúistís', a deir an Garda, 'Tá coinníoll damanta eile freisin ann, a Ghiúistís, ach b'fhearr liom gan tagairt dó anois, ar fhaitíos go mbainfeadh sé gáire amach. Beidh mé ag iarraidh cead an cás a chur siar go dtí ...'

'Drochrath air!' a smaoinigh an Giúistís, amach as ard. Ansin, i ngnáthbhealach cainte: 'Cé leis a mbaineann an coinníoll seo atá i gceist agat?'

'Le hAcht na gCoireanna Speisialta, a Ghiúistís.'

'Cuirfear siar an cás go dtí an Chúirt Speisialta ag meán lae INNIU,' a dúirt an Giúistís. 'An chéad chás eile!'

* * * * *

'Síos, síos. Síos,' a dúirt an Garda.

Sea. Chuaigh mé, muid síos ar ais an staighre céanna go dtí an halla fada. Suas liom, linn ar ais staighre eile a thug muid go cillín eile. Casadh an eochair, osclaíodh an doras. Dúradh liom a dhul isteach. Dúnadh an doras. Bhí mé faoi ghlas aríst. Bhí fear eile ann romham. Chrom mé mo cheann ag beannú dhó. Fear breá téagartha lách a bhí ann, le súil dhubh is gan mórán slachta ar a chulaith éadaigh. Baile Átha Cliathach, déarfainn.

'Muise, cén chaoi a bhfuil tú ar chor ar bith, a dhuine bhoicht,' a dúirt sé, mar dhuine a raibh aithne aige orm. Ach b'fhéidir gur bheannaigh sé mar sin do chuile dhuine. 'Teann anuas ag an tine go dtéifidh do chosa.'

'An cara leat mé?'

'Sea, go cinnte,' a dúirt sé. 'Bíonn chuile dhuine muinteartha le chéile i bpálás mar seo. Nach fíor dhom é? Agus inis seo dhom, céard atá déanta agat?'

'Tada,' a dúirt mé, 'beagnach tada.'

'Is tusa an fear ceart,' a dúirt sé. 'An aisteoir tú ... nó amadán, deargamadán, ar nós mise?'

Níor fhreagair mé. Bhí an t-ábhar ró-dhomhain dhom an tráth seo den mhaidin.

'An bhfuil aon imní ort faoi Chúirt an Mheán Lae?' a d'fhiafraigh mé dhe.

'Bhoil, bhoil,' a dúirt sé, 'd'fhéadfaí a rá gurb í an chúirt is measa ar an domhan í, an chúirt is lú trua, gan ceart ná cóir le fáil inti. Giúistís a bhfuil ainm Gaeilge air—má bhíonn sé sin ann, seans maith go bhfaighimid príosún saoil.'

'Tá imní ort mar sin?'

'Á bhoil,' a dúirt sé, agus thosaigh sé ag cantaireacht leis, mar seo:

'Má bhíonn imní ort, gheobhaidh tú bás, is caithfidh muid thú a chur,

Mura mbeidh imní ort, gheobhaidh tú bás, is caithfidh muid thú a chur,

Ach mo chomhairle dhuit, a bheith ar nós chuile dhuine, mar dhea

Is bí ag gabháil fhoinn go M.A.I.D.I.N. ... inn ...'

'Agus tá cuid eile freisin ann, tá a fhios agat. Níl agamsa ach giotaí de, níor chuala mé ach uair nó dhó é, i mo chloigeann fhéin. B'fhiú dhuit é a chloisteáil canta mar ba chóir. Tá sé thar barr, clasaiceach. Níor chuala muid a leithéid ariamh cheana.'

Thosaigh sé ag portaireacht dhó fhéin agus chas sé abairt nó dhó. Bhí glór breá aige. Rinne sé dreas feadaíola freisin, sách ceolmhar. Lig sé a scíth ansin.

'Tá siad le Seán a thabhairt ormsa,' a dúirt mise, 'ceapann said go bhfeileann sé dhom.'

'Tá sé sin fíorbharúil,' a dúirt sé, 'tá siad ag glaoch Breandán ormsa—ceapann siad go bhfeileann sé dhom.'

Bhí sé ag cuimhniú air féin.

'Casfaidh mé píosa d'amhrán breá eile dhuit,' a dúirt sé, 'sula dtiocfaidh siad siúd isteach aríst le deireadh a chur leis an spraoi. Amhrán é seo faoi éan cáiliúil, "An Bonnán Buí", as an traidisiún Gaelach. Is é naomhphátrún na n-éan ar fuaid an domhain é, ach níl agamsa ach cúpla smut de:

''Sí mo stór a dúirt liom ligean den ól

Nó go ngiorróinn mo shaol fhéin ó bhliain go bliain

Ach is mé fhéin a dúirt léi gurb é a choinníonn beo mé

Is mura bhfaighidh mé deár dhe, beidh an ceol ar ceal.'

Thug mé bualadh bos dhó. Agus thug sé bualadh bos dhó fhéin.

Bhí mé ag éirí tuirseach ag éisteacht leis—mar bhí mé tuirseach.

Sul i bhfad, áfach, bhí an rud a bhí ar tí tarlú, ag tarlú. D'oscail an doras, mháirseáil dhá Gharda isteach agus mháirseáil siad 'Breandán' amach leo. Nuair a bhí sé ag imeacht, chas sé timpeall agus meangadh mór cairdiúil air, chaoch sé an tsúil orm go fíor-rógánta.

'Go n-éirí an t-ádh leat, a mhic ó,' a dúirt sé. 'Ná déan rud ar bith a dhéanfainnse!' agus d'imigh as amharc, é fhéin agus an dá Gharda.

D'airigh mé uaigneach ina dhiaidh. Níl fhios agam céard a d'éirigh dhó ina dhiaidh sin.

I m'aonar aríst, ar feadh píosa. Ach ní píosa fada é.

* * * * *

An doras á oscailt. Mise a bhí uathu an iarraidh seo. Baineadh siúl aríst asam—síos agus suas staighrí agus an scéal céanna uilig, ar ais aríst. Nó gur tháinig muid go dtí staighre cloch a bhí ag dul in airde go dtí an doras iarainn a bhí ar an gCúirt Speisialta. Mo Gharda liom.

Gardaí eile ann freisin lena dtréad, ina seasamh i líne rialta amháin.

Deineadh comhartha ordaitheach liom a dhul suas go dtí an doras mór. Isteach liom sa Chúirt—mo Gharda, chomh dílis le mo scáile, i mo dhiaidh aniar.

Ansin, cuireadh an t-iontas is mó a cuireadh ariamh orm: cé a bhí ann ach Dónall Ó Conaill breá é féin, le taobh an Ghiúistís. Ní ina sheasamh a bhí sé, ach ina shuí—go han- socair, agus ó chaitheas mé é a rá, go huasal, chomh státúil le huachtarán tíre.

Tháinig feairín beag tanaí go dtí mé. Bhí péire spéacláirí tiubha air agus bileoga oifigiúla ina láimh aige. Bhí uaireadóir mór ar shlabhra ar crochadh óna veist. Ní thabharfá samhail ar bith dhó ach fear bréige sa ngort. Ní raibh cuma ró-shásta ar chor ar bith air.

'Mise a labhras ar do shon', a dúirt sé. 'Is mise do dhlíodóir. Ní déarfaidh tusa tada ach a admháil go bhfuil tú ciontach, má labhrann an Giúistís leat. NÁ DÉAN DEARMAD, fág an chaint fúmsa. Tá cleachtadh agam orthu seo. Seo í an Chúirt Speisialta. Ainm Gaeilge atá ar an nGiúistís seo inniu! Níl agat ach seans dona. Ach, go n-éirí leat.'

'Tuigim,' a dúirt mise, ach níor thuigeas. 'Cé hé an duine uasal atá ina shuí le taobh an Ghiúistís?'

Bhí a fhios agam cé a bhí ann, ach le bheith cinnte dearfa ...

'Ó,' a deir sé, 'sin é Dónall Binn é féin,' a dúirt an dlíodóir.

'Cén chaoi ar thugadar ann é?' a d'fhiafraigh mé de.

'An Brainse Speisialta, ar ndóigh, deineann siad rudaí mar sin, gan stró ar bith.'

Buaileadh cnag na Cúirte.

* * * * *

'Céard í an chúis in aghaidh an fhir seo?' a d'fhiafraigh an Giúistís.

'Tá cúig chúis ann ar fad, a Ghiúistís,' a dúirt mo Gharda.

'Céard iad?'

'Aon: Maslú do cheannaire Stáit i Sráid Uí Chonaill, Ceantar Uirbeach Bhaile Átha Cliath.'

'Dó: Ionsaí ar cheannaire Stáit ag an ionad céanna.'

'Trí:. Ionsaí ar oifigí an Stáit ag an ionad céanna.'

'Ceathair:. A bheith i seilbh airm chontúirteach.'

'Cúig: Cur in aghaidh é a ghabháil.'

'An bhfuil an cosantóir ag pléadáil ciontach nó neamh-chiontach?' a d'fhiafraigh an Giúistís.

Labhair mise amach: 'Neamhchiontach.'

Chuir an Giúistís a lámh lena chluais, cosúil le duine nach mbeadh éisteacht ró-mhaith aige.

'Céard atá sé a rá', a d'fhiafraigh sé de mo dhlíodóir.

'Ciontach, a Ghiúistís'

'An raibh aon chúis ina aghaidh roimhe seo?'

'Ní raibh, a Ghiúistís. Is cinnte nach dtéann sé lena dhea-thréithe coireanna uafásacha mar seo a dhéanamh. Téann sé in aghaidh gach ní a seasann sé dóibh, agus an dea-cháil atá air. Iarraim go humhal ort é a scaoileadh saor faoin Acht Promhaidh, agus ...'

Bhris an Giúistís isteach air. 'Céard seo? É a ligean saor? Lenár gCeannairí Stáit, agus Dianna Uaisle ár sinsir, ar nós an laoich uasail atá inár measc inniu le caoinchead agus sárobair an Bhrainse Speisialta, a mhaslú? An tAcht Promhaidh ab ea?'

Ansin, ag breathnú amach thar a chuid spéacláirí ormsa agus ansin ar mo dhlíodóir, a bhí, dála an scéil, ar creathadh ina chraiceann—ar fhaitíos go gcaillfeadh sé a phost agus a phinsean agus go mbeadh sé fágtha fuar dealbh ar shráideanna Bhaile Átha Cliath, cheap mé.

'Dhera!' a dúirt an Giúistís, ag léiriú a raibh go domhain ina chroí—de dhéistean, dímheas, eascairdeas, in aon fhocal gáifeach amháin. 'Ní fiú faic an tAcht Promhaidh sa Chúirt seo agamsa. Ar Acht na gCoireanna Speisialta a bhíonn muid ag caint anseo. Tuigeann tú?'

'Tuigim, a Ghiúistís, ach ...'

'Príosún saoil', a deir an Giúistís go tobann, ag bualadh an chasúir go dúshlánach, ag baint geit asainn ar fad, agus as Ó Conaill féin, a bhí go ciúin, socair, smaointeach go dtí sin.

Bhí mise ag cuimhniú, nó ag iarraidh a bheith ag cuimhniú, ar na mionnaí móra le liodán acu a scaoileadh amach, tharla nach raibh aon sásamh eile agam—ach bhíodar ag súil leis is cosúil. Bhíodar an-scioptha ar a gcosa. Go tobann d'airigh mé mar a bheadh tuáille fáiscthe ar mo bhéal ...

Tarraingíodh síos an staighre mí-ásach sin mé. Ansin síos staighre eile, fiú amháin, chomh domhain is a bhí ann go dtí áit gan ainm. Buaileadh sa chloigeann mé. Ansin, tháinig codladh orm—de bharr an bhuille.

In a Pickle
Dara Ó Conaola

It was Daniel O'Connell who caused me the greatest misfortune of all—much as he is admired and praised by all the clans, and even if some people worship him like a god. It is true that I greatly admired him myself, too. I would have done anything in my power and half as much again to defend his honour, any time. I surely would—until that night.

* * * * *

'Where was I, did you say?'

'You were in the city, of course.'

'Yes, but where exactly?'

'Oh! You were in the pub. Your regular haunt. You had spent a long afternoon there.'

'Where did I go then?'

'Suddenly, you announced you were leaving. Nothing would hold you back. You left. I don't remember anything else about you.'

* * * * *

Since we're unable to remember, I doubt if we can ever discover where I went after leaving ye. But this much is certain, I must have gone to a couple of places during the time you have recorded. I must have spent the time somewhere, for I never heard of a portion of time slipping away out of life without being spent somehow, somewhere.

I must have detoured my way down by Trinity College. A wide bridge loomed large ahead of me: O'Connell Bridge, named after the most celebrated Gaeilgeoir[1] ever, Daniel O'Connell. As everyone knows, it is the Irish language that saved his life once upon a time during his eventful life.

---

[1] An Irish speaker.

'Daniel O'Connell, do you understand Irish?' asked an Irish waitress serving at one of the longest tables in London at the time.

'And what is it that you have noticed, my girl from Ireland?' he asked in Irish, totally carefree and suspecting nothing, as I was this night.

'Well, I would have you know that there is enough poison in your cup that would kill a hundred people!'

Nobody else present understood the words. But O'Connell was smart. He knew what to say:

'Can I have a glass of water instead, please?'

He survived the danger.

It's a long time since I heard Johnny D'Arcy telling that story.

'It is true indeed that it's her, the Irish language that saved him,' Johnny said.

God be good to him and also to the girl from Ireland, O'Connell—and me.

I remember the bridge. There was nobody about. There were no cars to be seen, buses, or any moving objects. Only one wide bridge, lonely and calm. All lit up, nicely.

O'Connell himself, of course, was there. With his guardian angels.

I greeted him merrily and cordially, as is truly my nature. It must have been Irish or English I used, as my knowledge of Latin, French, Greek or the language of the seagulls is pretty poor.

However, whatever language I used, it did not impress the great man.

I might as well say it, here and now, there is nothing in this world that maddens me more than this kind of arrogance, this type of dumb indifference from anybody—I mean nobody. No matter who she is. Or what he is.

I didn't expect him to say much, being a stone man and all. But he could at least pretend. There are so many ways to do things when you're stuck. He could have discreetly whispered directly to my heart, for my heart is always opened to receive a kind message. He could have said he had heard what I said, that he was glad to hear it, thanks, go on home now like a good man, to your wife, and children if you're married ... but if you're only a student, go back to your bedsitter and study your books ... and leave me alone here on my lofty pedestal. That's what he should have said. But, alas! No, not a syllable in any language and I felt so let down; dejected, betrayed.

Despite that, being the patient man that I am and, also, since a couple of wise old proverbs happened to pop into my head, I thought that I should give O'Connell another chance.

'Good evening, Dan,' I said, 'and God and Mary be with you this pleasant hour.'

If I might say so myself, I used the clearest and sweetest Irish you could ever ask for, as pure as the Irish once spoken by my grandparents. And that's saying something.

But, all to no avail. I came to the conclusion if I had, even, spoken the Irish Brian Boru spoke, O'Connell would not budge. The haughty, stubborn mule.

After that, things went downhill altogether between us. My admiration had suddenly turned into fury. The clear calm night air was turning into an angry sky.

'God damn blast you up there, if that's the way you want it!' I shouted up to him, getting ready to give him a piece of my mind, to take him down a peg, who did he think he was anyway, so proudly up there with his head in the city skyline. I would tell him that, too.

I faced up to him. It was rather audacious of me, I admit. For anyone there to see me, I'm sure I would have appeared aggressive and agitated or to put it mildly—unruly.

But, very quickly, I was encircled by a very orderly lot indeed, closing in on me from all sides. Sturdy, stern, strong-armed men. Trouble.

I drew my noble sword.

'Drop the sword in the name of the law!' shouted one of them in a commanding voice.

'You stay clear of me,' I shouted back at him, adopting the same air of authority as he had.

'You have broken the law,' he said, 'we're under orders to take you into custody. You,' he said, 'have no choice in the matter.'

'You,' I said to him, 'are wrong, I am armed with a sword. I can fight.'

'We'll see about that then.'

'We will,' said I, 'and what's more, there are two sides to this conflict.'

'What on earth are you talking about? We are here to arrest you. There is no two ways about it. Don't be wasting our time.'

'This contest is between two people. If you want to save time, you arrest the other fellow as well,' I said, pointing up to O'Connell. 'It's then and only then that I'll agree to go peacefully.'

He paused and looked around at the other men. They communicated silently in a strange non-verbal language, for about a minute. I didn't understand one word of their strange, hushed murmuring.

'Let me explain,' he said, in a slightly different tone of voice, somewhat friendlier, I thought. 'We will arrest O'Connell also, provided you put down your, um, the sword and come with us peacefully. We are the law, we will treat you well. What do you say?'

'But can I trust you?'

'Yes, you can. We are honest peacemakers, we strictly adhere to protocol. I personally give you my word of honour on that. How is that?'

'Will you swear to it in the presence of all those gathered here, including the angels?'

He nodded a 'yes'.

He then went down on one knee and swore to me and to everyone else that he'd keep his word. For that reason, I dropped my lovely Cú Chulainn sword that I had won some time ago at a Feis Ceoil for coming first in a step dancing competition.

* * * * *

As soon as that happened, another thing happened—and I wasn't too pleased about it.

The circle of stern strong-armed men lunged towards me. They grabbed me everywhere with their strong hands. One caught me by the ear. They lifted me clear off the ground. Then they pushed me into a big motorcar, better known as the Black Maria, with my hands tied behind my back. I was captured.

Black Maria went off at an alarming speed.

O'Connell was left on his pedestal, proud and free.

Well, so much for their word of honour, I thought. I was set alight with indignation. I felt hard done by. Oh! I was so angry.

'Your law is crooked,' I said.

There was no response.

'And you're a very crooked lot of scoundrels. As crooked as you look. As stupid as you look.'

A thump in the ribs and a shower of curses was their retort.

I repeated some of their curses back at them. They were quick to inform me that an extra charge would be brought against me for swearing!

'Well, if that's the case, I might as well earn them,' I said.

Every bad word I heard since I left home, I recited like a litany, for which I got a nice 'pray for us' in the ribs for each one. Some words annoyed them more than others. Calling one of them a 'Twit' earned me double pay. 'Gurrier' is another one that annoyed them greatly. But the one that angered them most was a 'Black and Tan'. So I kept repeating them to pass the time. So, in no time at all we had arrived at the station, as they called it; barracks, I call it.

By now I was getting tired and weary, as the lack of food and drink started to have an effect on me.

I remember the barracks. I was dragged in to the inner room. A chair was waiting for me.

A voice emanated from the four corners of the ceiling, all at the same time: 'Please be seated!'

I obeyed.

Two men sat in front of me and one behind. Our little interview then began.

'Can you confirm your name is John that was given to us by your generous drinking pal, known as The Cop— for obvious reasons,' lowering his voice and addressing the fellow behind me. 'Is that your name?'

I played dumb.

'What have you got in your pockets?'

I remained dumb.

'Are you a member of an illegal organization?'

Dumb.

I felt I had a bit of the upper hand on them now and that I would remain in control as long as I didn't give them any information. This gave me a little of my self-confidence back.

'Even if I had committed a crime, you could never build a case against me asking those silly questions, you stupid git, you ...'

'Who are you calling a pig?'

'I wouldn't call you a pig,' I said, 'the pig is a noble animal. Not like you.'

One of them couldn't take that from me and hit me a nasty clatter across the face.

This conversation continued for an hour at least. Questions, pushing, thumping, questions.

But I told them nothing.

* * * * *

Then, at last, they brought me down to a cell. I was given a blanket and ordered to go to sleep. I gladly consented.

I was about to fall asleep on my nice hard wooden bench when I heard someone coming back. Oh no!

Oh! But, yes! It was somebody new. A middle-aged man, more civil looking than the others, I thought. He was nice enough to me, too. But this wouldn't fool me. I hadn't forgotten the way they had tricked me about arresting O'Connell also.

I also knew that I wouldn't get a minute's peace from them if I didn't cooperate somehow. So I said to the nice middle-aged civil man:

'Look. I will not give you any information now, tonight, but in the morning, if O'Connell is arrested as was agreed, I promise I'll give you all the information you require.'

'Um,' he said.

I was hoping that 'um' meant 'yes'; that he would be happy he got even that amount of co-operation, for the time being. He thought for a minute, before he spoke.

'Ok,' he said. He got up suddenly and went off.

I don't remember anything else about that.

* * * * *

Morning came with the dawn. Court, I realized, was my concern now. I decided I'd go with the predictable flow, anyhow. It was the only course of action opened to me.

I was waiting since dawn, being dragged from one cell to another. 'The waiting was the worst part.' Is my life being reduced to a mere cliché!

I was brought to a cell in the courthouse. There were two traveller friends of mine there before me. There were three wooden benches. I sat on one of them. The door opened and a man arrived with tea. My two friends got up quickly to avail of the hospitality. A tin cup of tea and a slice of bread. One was placed beside me. I decided that I'd go on hunger strike, at least, for the time being. So, I got up and gave a good kick to the tea and bread and sent them flying.

The poor guard said nothing, but I could hear him thinking: 'I'll bear that in mind … to be added to his account of charges. I'm just doing my job.' I was getting used to that non-verbal lingo by now. I felt that the morning guards were nicer than the night guys.

I waited. And in due course, I was called …

* * * * *

I was escorted down to the basement. There was a long hall. A stone staircase stood at one end of the hall and the guard told me to stand there and wait for further instructions; which we did, for a minute, or two, I suppose …

'Get up them steps,' instructed the guard to me.

I did. We did.

So, we entered the courtroom. I was directed to my stand. The judge was sitting in front of me and a clerk beside him. Another clerk was there too, sitting in front of them. A row of clerks lined each wall of the courtroom. Another group of men and women stood at the back, all dressed up in the latest fashion. I thought they were spectators.

'So, this is the one with no name,' said the judge.

'There is an awkward condition also, Judge,' said the guard, 'but I'd rather not say it out loud for fear it might make the people laugh, Judge. I will be asking to put the case back for a while ...'

'Damn it!' thought the judge aloud. Then in an ordinary tone: 'To whom this particular condition refers?'

'It concerns the Special Criminal Act, Judge.'

'This case is adjourned to a hearing in the Special Court at midday, TODAY,' said the Judge. 'Next case!'

* * * * *

'Down. Go down,' said the guard.

So he, we, retraced our steps downwards and landed on the stone floor of the long hall once more. We then went back up the stairs that led us to another cell. The door of the cell was then unlocked and opened. I was told to enter. I did. I was locked up again. Another man was there before me. I nodded to him as a greeting. He was a stocky friendly man with a black eye and an unkempt appearance. A Dublin man, I thought.

'Wisha, how are you at all, me ould flower,' he said, with a certain familiarity, as if we had met before somewhere. But, maybe he greeted everybody like that. 'Come up to the fire, where you ought to be!'

'Are you a friend of mine?'

'Of course, I am,' he said, 'we're all friends when we share this parlour, right!'

I nodded a vague nod.

'So, tell me, what did you do?' he said.

'Nothing,' I said, 'nothing much.'

'You're the right man,' he said. 'Are you an actor, or ... are you an *amadán*, a damn fool like me?'

I didn't answer. It was too philosophical for me at this time of the morning.

'Are you worried about the Midday Court?' I asked him then.

'Well, well,' he said, 'it's only the worst court in the world, with no mercy, no justice. And there is an ould judge who writes his name in Irish and if he is there today we'll get life for sure.'

'So you're worried?'

'Ah, well,' he said, paused, and began to rhyme off, like this:

'"If you worry, you'll die, and we'll have to bury you,

And, if you don't worry you'll die, and we'll have to bury you,

So, if you take my advice, you will act as you were normal

And sing away till M.O.R.N.I.N.G ... ing ..."

'And, there's more to that. But I only know bits of it. I only heard it once or twice ... in my own head. You would want to hear it sung properly. I tell you, it's a beauty. It's classical. Out of this world it is.'

He started to hum to himself and he sang a couple of words. He had a big voice. He whistled a bit too, in tune. Then he rested for a bit.

'They are going to call me John,' I said, 'they think it suits me.'

'That's bleeding funny,' he said, 'they are calling me Brendan—they think it suits me.'

He was thinking.

'I'll sing you a verse of another great song,' he said, 'before they come again to spoil the fun. It is about a famous bird in the Irish tradition. It is "The Yellow Bittern", the patron saint of all the birds in the world, I have only scraps of it:

'"It's my darling who told me to drink no more
Or that my life would be shortened by many a mile
But it is me who told her that the drink keeps me going
And if I don't get a drink soon—I will end this song."'

I applauded him. And he applauded himself.

I was beginning to get tired listening to him—because I was tired.

But soon enough, the next thing that was about to happen, happened. The door opened, two guards came in and marched poor 'Brendan' out with them. As he was leaving, he turned around and gave me a big smile and winked like a real rogue.

'Good look, son,' he said to me. 'Don't do anything I would do!' as he disappeared, along with the two guards.

I felt sad when he left. I don't know what has become of him.

I was on my own again for a while. But not for a long while.

* * * * *

The door opened. It was my turn. I was put through my paces once more—down and up and what have you. Until we arrived at the stone stairs that led to the iron door of the Special Court. My guard was with me.

There were other guards there too with their flock, all in an orderly line.

I got the call, signal, to go up to the big door. I entered the court, my guard following me closely, as faithful as my shadow.

Twas then I got the greatest surprise of my life: there was Daniel O'Connell, himself sitting beside the judge. Not standing, but seated—very still, and if I may say so, very dignified and presidential.

A thin man came to me. He wore thick glasses and he carried a bunch of papers. A big watch on a chain was hanging from his inner garment. He looked for all the world like a scarecrow I knew one time. He was far from happy.

'I will speak on your behalf,' he said. 'I'm your solicitor. You'll say nothing except to say that you are pleading guilty if you're asked by the judge. REMEMBER, leave the talking to me. I know these people. This is the Special Court. The judge today goes by the Irish version of his name! I don't think you have much of a chance. But, good luck.'

'I see,' I said. But I didn't see. 'Who is that big shot sitting next to the judge?'

I knew who it was, but just to be absolutely sure …

'Oh, good God, that's Gentleman Dan himself,' said the solicitor.

'How did they manage to bring him here?' I asked.

'That's the work of the Special Branch, they'll stop at nothing.'

The court bell rang.

'Here we go, here we go,' my solicitor repeated; once for me, once for him.

* * * * *

'What is the charge against this man?' asked the judge.

'There are five charges in all, Judge,' said my guard.

'Well, what are they?'

'One: insulting a head of state at O'Connell Street, Dublin Metropolitan District.

'Two: An attack on a head of state at the same location.

'Three: An attack on officers of the state at same location

'Four: In possession of a dangerous weapon.

'Five: Resisting arrest.'

'Is the defendant pleading guilty or not guilty?' the judge asked.

I spoke up: 'Not guilty.'

The judge put his hand to his ear, like someone who was hard of hearing.

'What is that he is saying?' he asked my solicitor.

'Guilty, Judge.'

'Had he ever been in court before now?'

'No, Judge. It is totally out of character for him to be involved in this type of appalling behaviour. It goes against everything he stands for and his good reputation. I humbly appeal to you, Judge, to let him go free under the Probation Act, and ...'

The judge interrupts him: 'What? Let him go free? To insult our state leaders and our own noble gods, our ancestry, like the great and wonderful hero we have here sitting amongst us today, thanks to the great and ingenious work of our own Special Branch. The Probation Act, you say?'

Then, looking over his glasses at me and then at my solicitor who was, by the way, shivering and sweating at this stage—afraid he would lose his job or his pension and that he'd be left penniless on the streets of Dublin, I suppose.

'Yerrah!' the judge said, expressing his inner most feeling—his disgust, disapproval, disagreement, all contained in that one word. 'The Probation Act does not apply at all, at all, here in my court. I only deal with cases relating to the Special Criminal Act. You understand?'

'I do, Judge, but ...'

'Life imprisonment!' said the judge, suddenly banging his special hammer hard on the countertop. Giving us all a fright. Even startling the up-to-now cool, calm and calculated Mr O'Connell.

I was thinking, or rather trying to think, of some atrocious abusive language I would fire at the judge, since I had no other bit of defence left—but they were one step ahead of me. They were really quick. A towel was tightened across my mouth. Then, dragged down those dreadful stairs one more time. And even down another stairs, way down deep to a place that has no name. I was given a blow to the head. Then I went to sleep—as a result of the blow.

Two More Gallants

William Trevor

You will not, I believe, find either Lenehan or Corley still parading the streets of Dublin, but often in the early evening a man called Heffernan may be found raising a glass of Paddy in Toner's public house; and FitzPatrick, on his bicycle, every working day makes the journey across the city, from Ranelagh to the offices of McGibbon, Tait & FitzPatrick, solicitors and commissioners for oaths. It is on his doctor's advice that he employs this mode of transport. It is against the advice of *his* that Heffernan continues to indulge himself in Toner's. The two men no longer know one another. They do not meet and, in order to avoid a confrontation, each has been known to cross a street.

Thirty or so years ago, when I first knew Heffernan and FitzPatrick, the relationship was different. The pair were closely attached, Heffernan the mentor, FitzPatrick ready with a laugh. All three of us were students, but Heffernan, a Kilkenny man, was different in the sense that he had been a student for as long as anyone could remember. The College porters said they recalled his presence over fifteen years and, though given to exaggeration, they may well have been accurate in that: certainly Heffernan was well over thirty, a small ferrety man, swift to take offence.

FitzPatrick was bigger and more amiable. An easy smile perpetually creased the bland ham of his face, causing people to believe, quite incorrectly, that he was stupid. His mouse-coloured hair was kept short enough not to require a parting, his eyes reflected so profound a degree of laziness that people occasionally professed surprise to find them open. Heffernan favoured pin-striped suits, FitzPatrick a commodious blue blazer. They drank in Kehoe's in Anne Street.

'He is one of those chancers,' Heffernan said, 'we could do without.'

'Oh, a right old bollocks,' agreed FitzPatrick.

'"Well, Mr Heffernan,"' he says, '"I see you are still with us."'

'As though you might be dead.'

'If he had his way.'

In the snug of Kehoe's they spoke of Heffernan's *bête noire*, the aged Professor Flacks, a man from the North of Ireland.

'"I see you are still with us,"' Heffernan repeated. 'Did you ever hear the beat of that?'

'Sure, Flacks is senile.'

'The mots in the lecture giggle when he says it.'

'Oh, an ignorant bloody crowd.'

Heffernan became meditative. Slowly he lit a Sweet Afton. He was supported in his continuing studentship by the legacy left to him for that purpose by an uncle in Kilkenny, funds which would cease when he was a student no longer. He kept that tragedy at bay by regularly failing the Littlego examination, a test of proficiency in general studies to which all students were obliged to submit themselves.

'A fellow came up to me this morning,' he said now, 'a right eejit from Monasterevin. Was I looking for grinds in Littlego Logic? Five shillings an hour.'

FitzPatrick laughed. He lifted his glass of stout and drank from it, imposing on his upper lip a moustache of foam which was permitted to remain there.

'A minion of Flacks,' Heffernan continued. 'A Flacks boy and no mistake, I said to myself.'

'You can tell them a mile off.'

'"I know your father," I said to him. "Doesn't he deliver milk?" Well, he went the colour of a sunset. "Avoid conversations with Flacks," I told him. "He drove a wife and two sisters insane."'

'Did your man say anything?'

'Nothing, only "Cripes".'

'Oh Flacks is definitely peculiar,' FitzPatrick agreed.

In point of fact, at that time FitzPatrick had never met Professor Flacks. It was his laziness that caused him to converse in a manner which suggested he had, and it was his laziness also which prevented him from noticing the intensity of Heffernan's grievance. Heffernan hated Professor Flacks with a fervour, but in his vague and unquestioning way FitzPatrick assumed that the old professor was no more than a passing thorn in his friend's flesh, a nuisance that could be exorcized by means of complaint and abuse. Heffernan's pride did not at that time appear to play a part; and FitzPatrick, who knew his friend as well as anyone did, would not have designated him as a possessor of that quality to an unusual degree. The opposite was rather implied by the nature of his upkeep and his efforts not to succeed in the Littlego examination. But pride, since its presence might indeed be questioned by these facts, came to its own support: when the story is told in Dublin today it is never forgotten that it has its roots in Professor Flacks's causing girls to giggle because he repeatedly made a joke at Heffernan's expense.

Employed by the University to instruct in certain aspects of literature, Professor Flacks concentrated his attention on the writings of James Joyce, Shakespeare, Tennyson, Shelley, Coleridge, Wilde, Swift, Dickens, Eliot, Trollope, and many another familiar name were all bundled away in favour of a Joycean scholarship that thirty or so years ago was second to none in Irish university life. Professor Flacks could tell you whom Joyce had described as a terrified YMCA man, and the date of the day on which he had written that his soul was full of decayed ambitions. He spoke knowledgably of the stale smell of incense, like foul flowerwater; and of flushed eaves and stubble geese.

'Inane bloody show-off,' Heffernan said nastily in Kehoe's.

'You'll see him out, Heff.'

'A bogs like that would last for ever.'

Twelve months later, after he and Heffernan had parted company, FitzPatrick repeated all that to me. I didn't know either of them well, but was curious because a notable friendship had so abruptly come to an end. FitzPatrick, on his own, was inclined to talk to anyone.

We sat in College Park, watching the cricket while he endeavoured to remember the order of subsequent events. It was Heffernan who'd had the idea, as naturally it would be, since FitzPatrick still knew Professor Flacks only by repute and had not suffered the sarcasm which Heffernan found so offensive. But FitzPatrick played a vital part in the events which followed, because the elderly woman who played the main part of all was a general maid in FitzPatrick's digs.

'Has that one her slates on?' Heffernan inquired one night as they passed her by in the hall.

'Ah, she's only a bit quiet.'

'She has a docile expression all right.'

'She wouldn't damage a fly.'

Soon after that Heffernan took to calling in at Fitz-Patrick's digs in Donnybrook more often than he had in the past. Sometimes he was there when FitzPatrick arrived back in the evening, sitting in the kitchen while the elderly maid pricked sausages or cut up bread for the meal that would shortly be served. Mrs Maginn, the landlady, liked to lie down for a while at that time of day, so Heffernan and the maid had the kitchen to themselves. But finding him present on several occasions when she came down-stairs, Mrs Maginn in passing mentioned the fact to her lodger. FitzPatrick, who didn't himself understand what Heffernan's interest in the general maid was, replied that his friend liked to await his return in the kitchen because it was warm. Being an easy-going woman, Mrs Maginn was appeased.

'There's no doubt in my mind at all,' Heffernan stated in Kehoe's after a few weeks of this behaviour. 'If old Flacks could hear it he'd have a tortoise's pup.'

FitzPatrick wagged his head, knowing that an explanation was in the air. Heffernan said: 'She's an interesting old lassie.'

He then told FitzPatrick a story which FitzPatrick had never heard before. It concerned a man called Corley who had persuaded a maid in a house in Baggot Street to do a small service for him. It concerned, as well, Corley's friend, Lenehan, who was something of a wit. At first FitzPatrick was confused by the story, imagining it to be about a couple of fellow-students whom he couldn't place.

'The pen of Jimmy Joyce,' Heffernan explained. 'That yarn is Flacks's favourite of the lot.'

'Well, I'd say there wasn't much to it. Sure, a skivvy never would.'

'She was gone on Corley.'

'But would she steal for him?'

'You're no romantic, Fitz.'

FitzPatrick laughed, agreeable to accepting this opinion. Then, to his astonishment, Heffernan said: 'It's the same skivvy Mrs Maginn has above in your digs.'

FitzPatrick shook his head. He told Heffernan to go on with himself, but Heffernan insisted.

'She told me the full story herself one night I was waiting for you—maybe the first night I ever addressed a word
to her. "Come into the kitchen outa the cold, Mr Heffernan," she says. D'you remember the occasion it was? Late
after tea, and you didn't turn up at all. She fried me an
egg.'

'But, holy Christ, man—'

'It was the same night you did well with the nurse from
Dundrum.'

FitzPatrick guffawed. A great girl, he said. He repeated a
few details, but Heffernan didn't seem interested.

'I was told the whole works in the kitchen, like Jimmy
Joyce had it out of her when she was still in her teens. A
little gold sovereign was all she fecked for your man.'

'But the poor old creature is as honest as the day's long.'

'Oh, she took it all right and she still thinks Corley was
top of the bill.'

'But Corley never existed—'

'Of course he did. Wasn't he forever entertaining that
fine little tart with the witticisms of Master Lenehan?'

The next thing that happened, according to Fitz-
Patrick, was that a bizarre meeting took place. Heffernan
approached Professor Flacks with the information that the
model for the ill-used girl in Joyce's story 'Two Gallants'
had come to light in a house in Donnybrook. The Professor displayed considerable excitement, and on a night

when Mrs Maginn was safely at the pictures he was met by Heffernan at the bus stop and led to the kitchen.

He was a frail man in a tweed suit, not at all as FitzPatrick had imagined him. Mrs Maginn's servant, a woman of about the same age, was slightly deaf and moved slowly according to rheumatism. Heffernan had bought half a pound of fig-roll biscuits which he arranged on a plate. The old woman poured tea.

Professor Flacks plied her with questions. He asked them gently, with courtesy and diplomacy, without any hint of the tetchiness described so often by Heffernan. It was a polite occasion in the kitchen, Heffernan handing round the fig-rolls, the maid appearing to delight in recalling a romance in her past.

'And later you told Mr Joyce about this?' prompted Professor Flacks.

'He used to come to the house when I worked in North Frederick Street, sir. A dentist by the name of O'Riordan.'

'Mr Joyce came to get his teeth done?'

'He did, sir.'

'And you'd talk to him in the waiting-room, is that it?'

'I'd be lonesome, sir. I'd open the hall door when the bell rang and then there'd be a wait for maybe an hour before it'd ring again, sir. I recollect Mr Joyce well, sir.'

'He was interested in your—ah—association with the fellow you mentioned, was he?'

'It was only just after happening, sir. I was turned out of the place in Baggot Street on account of the bit of trouble. I was upset at the time I knew Mr Joyce, sir.'

'That's most understandable.'

'I'd often tell a patient what had happened to me.'

'But you've no hard feelings today? You were badly used by the fellow, yet—'

'Ah, it's long ago now, sir.'

Heffernan and FitzPatrick saw the Professor on to a bus and, according to FitzPatrick, he was quivering with pleasure. He clambered into a seat, delightedly talking to himself, not noticing when they waved from the pavement. They entered a convenient public house and ordered pints of stout.

'Did you put her up to it?' FitzPatrick inquired.

'The thing about that one, she'd do anything for a scrap of the ready. Didn't you ever notice that about her? She's a right old miser.'

It was that that Heffernan had recognized when first he'd paid a visit to Mrs Maginn's kitchen: the old maid was possessed of a meanness that had become obsessional with her. She spent no money whatsoever, and was clearly keen to add to whatever she had greedily accumulated. He had paid her a pound to repeat the story he had instructed her in.

'Didn't she say it well? Oh, top of the bill, I'd say she was.'

'You'd be sorry for old Flacks.'

'Oh, the devil take bloody Mr Flacks.'

Some months went by. Heffernan no longer visited the kitchen in Donnybrook, and he hardly spoke at all of Professor Flacks. In his lazy way FitzPatrick assumed that the falsehoods which had been perpetuated were the be-all and end-all of the affair, that Heffernan's pride—now clearly revealed to him—had somehow been satisfied. But then, one summer's afternoon while the two idled in Stephen's Green in the hope of picking up girls, Heffernan said: 'There's a thing on we might go to next Friday.'

'What's that?'

'Mr Flacks performing. The Society of the Friends of James Joyce.'

It was a public lecture, one of several that were to be delivered during a week devoted by the Society to the life and work of the author who was its *raison d' être*. The Society's members came from far afield: from the United States, Germany, Finland, Italy, Australia, France, England and Turkey. Learned academics mingled with the less learned enthusiasts. Mr James Duffy's Chapelizod was visited, and Mr Power's Dublin Castle. Capel Street and Ely Place were investigated, visits were made to the renowned Martello Tower, to Howth and to Pim's. Betty Bellezza was mentioned, and Val from Skibereen. The talk was all Joyce talk. For a lively week Joyce reigned in Dublin.

On the appointed evening FitzPatrick accompanied his friend to Professor Flacks's lecture, his premonitions suggesting that the occasion was certain to be tedious. He had no idea what Heffernan was up to, and wasn't prepared to devote energy to speculating. With a bit of luck, he hoped, he'd be able to have a sleep.

Before the main event a woman from the University of Washington spoke briefly about Joyce's use of misprints; a bearded German read a version of 'The Holy Office' that had only recently been discovered. Then the tweeded figure of Professor Flacks rose. He sipped at a tumbler of water, and spoke for almost an hour about the model for the servant girl in the story, 'Two Gallants'. His discovery of that same elderly servant, now employed in a house in Donnybrook, engendered in his audience a whisper of excitement that remained alive while he spoke, and exploded into applause when he finished. A light flush enlivened the paleness of his face as he sat down. It was, as Heffernan remarked to his dozy companion, the old man's finest hour.

It was then that FitzPatrick first became uneasy. The packed lecture-hall had accepted as fact all that had been stated, yet none of it was true. Notes had been taken, questions were now being asked. A voice just behind the two students exclaimed that this remarkable discovery was worth coming two thousand miles to hear about. Mental pictures of James Joyce in a dentist's waiting-room flashed about the hall. North Frederick Street would be visited tomorrow, if not tonight.

'I'd only like to ask,' Heffernan shouted above the hub-bub, 'if I may, a simple little question.' He was on his feet. He had caught the attention of Professor Flacks, who was smiling benignly at him. 'I'd only like to inquire,' Heffernan continued, 'if the whole thing couldn't be a lot of baloney.'

'Baloney?' a foreign voice repeated.

'Baloney?' said Professor Flacks.

The buzz of interest hadn't died down. Nobody was much interested in the questions that were being asked except the people who were asking them. A woman near to FitzPatrick said it was extraordinarily moving that the ill-used servant girl, who had been so tellingly presented as an off-stage character by Joyce, should bear no grudge all these years later.

'What I mean, Professor Flacks,' said Heffernan, 'is I don't think James Joyce ever attended a dentist in North Frederick Street. What I'm suggesting to you, sir, is that the source of your information was only looking for a bit of limelight.'

FitzPatrick later described to me the expression that entered Professor Flacks's eyes. 'A lost kind of look,' he said, 'as though someone had poked the living daylights out of him.' The old man stared at Heffernan, frowning, not comprehending at first. His relationship with this student had been quite different since the night of the visit to Mrs Maginn's kitchen: it had been distinguished by a new friendliness, and what had seemed like mutual respect.

'Professor Flacks and myself,' continued Heffernan, 'heard the old lady together. Only I formed the impression that she was making the entire matter up. I thought, sir, you'd formed that opinion also.'

'Oh, but surely now, Mr Heffernan, the woman wouldn't do that.'

'There was never a dentist by the name of O'Riordan that practised in North Frederick Street, sir. That's a fact that can easily be checked.'

Heffernan sat down. An uneasy silence gripped the lecture-hall. Eyes turned upon Professor Flacks. Weakly, with a hoarseness in his voice, he said: 'But why, Mr Heffernan, would she have made all that up? A woman of that class would hardly have read the story, she'd hardly have known—'

'It's an unfortunate thing, sir,' interrupted Heffernan, standing up again, 'but that old one would do anything for a single pound note. She's of a miserly nature. I think what has happened,' he went on, his tone changing as he addressed the assembly, 'is that a student the Professor failed in an examination took the chance to get his own back. Our friend Jas Joyce,' he added, 'would definitely have relished that.'

In misery, Professor Flacks lifted the tumbler of water to his lips, his eyes cast down. You could sense him thinking, FitzPatrick reported, that he was a fool and he had been shown to be a fool. You could sense him thinking that he suddenly appeared to be unreliable, asinine and ridiculous. In front of the people who mattered to him most of all he had been exposed as a fraud he did not feel himself to be. Never again could he hold his head up among the Friends of James Joyce. Within twenty-four hours his students would know what had occurred.

An embarrassed shuffling broke out in the lecture-hall. People murmured and began to make their way into the aisles. FitzPatrick recalled the occasion in Mrs Maginn's kitchen, the two elderly puppets on the end of Heffernan's string, the fig-rolls and the tea. He recalled the maid's voice retailing the story that he, because he knew Heffernan so well, had doubted with each word that was uttered. He felt guilty that he hadn't sought the old man out and told him it wasn't true. He glanced through the throng in the lecture-hall at the lone figure in porridgy tweeds, and unhappily reflected that suicide had been known to follow such wretched disgrace. Outside the lecture-hall he told Heffernan to go to hell when a drink in Anne Street was suggested—a remark for which Heffernan never forgave him.

'I mean,' FitzPatrick said as we sat in College Park a long time later, 'how could anyone be as petty? When all the poor fellow ever said to him was "I see you are still with us?"'

I made some kind of reply. Professor Flacks had died a natural death a year after the delivery of his lecture on 'Two Gallants'. Earlier in his life he had not, as Heffernan had claimed, driven a wife and two sisters mad: he'd been an only child, the obituary said in the *Irish Times*, and a bachelor. It was an awkward kind of obituary, for the gaffe he'd made had become quite famous and was still fresh in Dubliners' minds.

We went on talking about him, FitzPatrick and I, as we watched the cricket in College Park. We spoke of his playful sarcasm and how so vehemently it had affected Heffernan's pride. We marvelled over the love that had caused a girl in the story to steal, and over the miserliness that had persuaded an old woman to be party to a trick. FitzPatrick touched upon his own inordinate laziness, finding a place for that also in our cobweb of human frailty.

The Black Church

Mary O'Donnell

Dublin, 24 April 1916

Ann Jane wiggled the doll's head, her two fingers lodged within the empty interior. She held up her hand and stared at the eyes. They flapped open as she bent her fingers slightly, then snapped shut again when she tilted her hand in the other direction. Her mother had gone down to Moore Street for a few herrings, leaving Ann Jane in charge of the Ba.

The Ba dragged herself along the floor on her bare bum. She was tethered around the waist with a thin leather leash which stretched to the leg of the table, around which it was knotted. She had a runny nose and a bad cold. Even so, she cooed pleasantly to herself, making swipes at Ann

Jane, whom she couldn't quite reach. Her chubby fingers stretched out again and again, as she grunted. Every so often the Ba gave a yowl of frustration. She would push herself forward, propping herself on both arms then arduously try to get her legs to lever her upright. But as much as she wanted to she couldn't walk yet.

Ann Jane ignored the Ba, glad of the relative quiet in the room. Her three brothers were below on the street. She knew that because, even three floors up, she recognized the gravelly shouts of the twins—Jimmy and Seán—and even the lighter, asthmatic rasp of Tomás. All three were older than Ann Jane.

She sighed and addressed the doll's head. 'If it wasn't for me you wouldn't be here, Belinda. You should be grateful I saved you from *Hell!*' she announced, giving the head a vigorous shake. She went on to describe the fire in the toyshop and what she saw the evening when she and Ma were on their way back from St Francis Xavier's Hall.

Ma used to bring Ann Jane to the moral meetings, even though, as she would tell her daughter, it was really Da who should be going to them. They had heard Fr Cullen talk about drink and depravity. His recommendations for avoiding drink and depravity had something to do with devotion to the Sacred Heart of Jesus, which would help even someone like Da to give up his ways and stop spending money they didn't have on porter and whiskey.

'So there we were, Belinda—Ma and me walking along after all the talk about the bad people drinking, when all of a sudden there's a WHOOSH ...'

She paused for effect and brought the doll's face quite close to her own, as if daring Belinda to contradict her. Her voice dropped menacingly. With every detail she shook Belinda's head even more, reminding her yet again of her good fortune in escaping death by fire.

Ma and Ann Jane had witnessed it all. Mr Morosini's toyshop had been embroiled and the whole premises destroyed. They had stopped to join the crowd of gawkers. They watched as a line was organized and firemen approached while buckets of water were launched into the air, in through the windows from which the glass had exploded, such was the terrible heat within. The street was roasting hot, the flames yellow and purple, sometimes green and blue, Ann Jane noted, but even worse was the violent sound from within.

Pop! Pop! Pop! She strained her ears. There it was again. *Pop! Pop-pop-pop-pop-pop-pop! Rata-tata-tata-tata! Pop-pop-pop!* Inside Mr Morosini's, lovely things were exploding or melting, or both, and the sound of the deaths of his dolls and teddies entered Ann Jane's ears like hot, painful needles.

'Ma,' she wailed, 'Mr Morosini's dollies are burning!'

She pitied the shop owner whose dolls were surely like his children, just as the one doll Ann Jane had was as real as the Ba, only better, because she never cried and was only slightly smelly.

For several years now she had pressed her face and nose up close to Mr Morosini's toyshop window. Sometimes she had wandered inside on her way home from school but the Italian had never encouraged her to dally. He would smile and gesture at his dolls and teddies, as if showing her his pride and joy, but then he would wag his forefinger at Ann Jane too. She disliked wagging fingers and shaking heads which characterized most interaction between older people and children. So she mostly stared in through the window, selecting the doll she would like best if God was as powerful as he was supposed to be and could grant your heart's desire.

Her heart's desire was for the dark-haired, ringleted doll called Prima Donna. Nobody had bought her. She sat, big and beautiful, on the middle shelf behind Mr Morosini's counter, surrounded by lesser dolls who came and went and were regularly replaced. But the Prima Donna's cheeks were peachy-pink, the rest of her face creamy, lips a cherry red, eyebrows delicate and her eyes the sweetest brown Ann Jane had ever seen. Once she asked Mr Morosini if the Prima Donna's eyelids opened and closed. In reply he had taken the doll from the shelf and perched her on the counter in front of Ann Jane. Gently he tilted Prima Donna backwards and her eyes snapped shut in deepest sleep. Ann Jane clapped her hands at this. Then he tilted Prima Donna forwards and her eyes were suddenly wide open, staring straight at Ann Jane.

On the night of the fire Ann Jane knew that the Prima Donna had also died, her lace and satin ruffles dissolved, her body streaming a fiery lava that joined the rest of the dying dolls as they flowed, melted in death's hot river. There was one more *Pop!* though, and something shot from the blazing premises and landed, smoking but not on fire, not far from Ma's feet. The other onlookers shifted, murmuring in surprise. Ann Jane made to run forward but Ma restrained her.

'Don't touch. It might burn you.'

'But Ma!'

'I said wait.'

Ma's hazel eyes observed the object for a moment, then she let go of Ann Jane's hand.

'Just be careful.'

Ann Jane hunkered down and poked at it with her forefinger. It was a doll's head. Not the Prima Donna's head, but one who had once been a Goldilocks and was now a little untidy looking. Her hair had not been entirely burned off. Ann Jane turned it carefully in both hands.

In fact the hair on the top of her head was untouched and only the long ringlets that would have hung down her back seemed to have been obliterated in the inferno. If Ma would trim the side curls the doll's head would be nice enough.

She called her Belinda. That night Da came home in good spirits and promised to make a raggedy body to fit Belinda's head and Ma promised to sew up some raggedy legs and arms. Her father's hands and face were filthy with coal dust; even between his teeth showed signs of coal. He had come from the docks with a hessian bag of lumps gathered along the road, between tram tracks, on the quays. He was sweating hard.

'We can blaze away for a few nights anyway if the weather turns cold,' he said with a smile, winking at Ma.

'I don't suppose you found anything to eat?' Ma stared at him with big eyes.

He shook his head slowly.

'Well there's nothing here, only what'd feed a mouse!' she snapped, throwing her hands up, then lowering them as quickly to her apron. Quickly she raised the apron to her face and moaned softly into it.

'Me belly's aching, that's the God's honest truth …'

All their bellies were aching. Ann Jane's belly bubbled, churned and twisted within her almost every day. She had reached a point where at times all she ever thought about was eating. As she and Belinda trailed along Sackville Street, or down Talbot Street, she rarely missed an opportunity to stare at the contents of the sweet shop windows. Her favourite was Kennedy's Bakery in Great Britain Street. She would stand outside it quite deliberately, just to smell the ooze of heat and yeast that wafted from the doorway as women shoppers passed in and out. Her eyes lit greedily on their square-wrapped boxes, in which nestled cakes and buns. Sometimes she fancied that even the smell of these delicious things was nourishment, could fill her up for an hour or two, to carry her as far as break-time at school. The nuns gave out batch loaf and jam at break to anyone who wanted it, with girls who spoke the best Irish getting slightly thicker slices, sometimes with country butter from the father of one of the young novices. For that reason Ann Jane was learning Irish very quickly.

In recent weeks the confectionary and bakery windows had gradually filled with Easter eggs—tantalizing ovals in various sizes. Kennedy's had also added chocolate eggs to its usual stock of bread and buns. She watched one day as a young man with protruding ears carefully placed an enormous egg right in the centre of the window, where it was surrounded, as if by admirers, by smaller eggs of various sizes. It was iced in scrolls of pink, blue and yellow, the words *Happy Easter 1916* done in white. The young man paused as he settled the egg, checking that his handiwork was stable on its supporting silvery stand, then glanced at Ann Jane. As usual, like many adults, he winked at her. She gave a small smile by way of response. It was beyond her why people felt the need to wink at childer like herself. It didn't change anything, although sometimes there was forgiveness in it, as if they, the childer, were not doing anything wrong after all. So often they were in the wrong and a wink, it was understood, conveyed an impression of kindness. After the young man had retreated into the shop she pressed her nose close to the window and peered in. Now the sweet scent of chocolate that lingered in the air from the half-open doorway contended with the yeasts and cooking odours she normally enjoyed.

'Do you want to come in?' a voice suddenly enquired.

She whirled around. It was the fellow with the big ears. She nodded, her eyes darting instinctively from ear to ear. One of them was slightly closer to the side of his head than the other, but it made little difference to the overall effect.

'Don't be shy,' he urged, holding open the door for her. As he did so, a hurrying, plump woman in a feathered hat wiggled around Ann Jane, brushing so close that the hard fabric of her mustard-yellow sleeve grazed her cheek. Ann Jane touched her face automatically and followed the man inside.

All was calm and orderly. For a moment the odour of baking and sweetness almost overwhelmed her and she hooked her fingers to the edge of the big counter, to steady herself.

'You'd like some chocolate, wouldn't you?'

'Yes please, mister.'

He reached beneath the counter and rummaged around before lifting up a white paper bag.

'We make mistakes in this place,' he confided. 'The chocolate breaks. Or the boss doesn't like the mix. This batch, for example,' he thrust a bag across the counter, 'is too sweet. So His Nibs says. I don't agree but I can't say as much.'

He shook his head and wiggled his eyebrows up and down.

'Why don't you tell him we like sweet things in Ireland?' Ann Jane sked cautiously.

The man regarded her soberly for a moment. 'Little Miss, I've told him once, but he doesn't listen. Since he's been to France, you see, he's been trying to convert his customers to bitter chocolate.'

Ann Jane wrinkled her nose at the thought. The man pushed the bag towards her again, nodding. She felt her heart flutter as she reached forward to grasp it. It was almost as good as the day Da came home with five pounds and ten shillings he'd won on a horse, when her heart had also fluttered and danced. Immediately, she ripped open the bag. There must have been nearly a pound of broken chocolate pieces.

'Now you'll be a good girl and not forget to share it?'

'Yes, mister,' she replied a little uncertainly.

'We should share everything, you know,' he added, but his eyes gleamed with mischief.

'Yes, mister.'

'Especially as we grow older. What age are you?'

'Ten and a half.'

He gave a light laugh. 'You won't be playing with that doll's head much longer then, will you?'

That was a strange thing to say, she thought, as she drifted slowly up Granby Street, munching and sucking. It was the most wonderful chocolate, silky and sweet as it dissolved around her teeth. At first she had gulped it down, but now, as her stomach filled, she could afford to slow up. Besides, she would have to keep a few pieces for the Ba. The boys were not getting any because they had not shared the sticks of Peggy's Leg that one of them had stolen from a Belvedere boy on his way home from school the previous year.

Easter, she imagined, would be like every other Easter she remembered, which were not very many, but were nevertheless marked by sameness and an absence of celebration. There would be early Mass, of course, with

Ma and the Ba and her brothers. Ma liked to talk about how the sun danced for sheer joy on the Dublin hills at Easter, on account of the Resurrection of Our Lord. It was understood by the children that Da might or might not attend Mass, depending on his state of health.

And it was as she had anticipated. Although not so hungry because they had had a broth of oxtail, carrots and barley in the middle of the day, followed by a strawberry jelly dessert from a package which one of the boys said was just lying on the street the day before, Easter was in every other respect unremarkable. Neither Ma nor Da had asked questions about the jelly and the whole family had enjoyed it, scooping precious spoonfuls from the blue delph basin in which it had been made. That afternoon, because of their meal, the room smelt different—there was saltiness and beefiness in the air as well as a hint of sweet strawberry. Everybody was in good humour, although the Ba kept coughing.

Even so, boredom set in very quickly after dinner and Ann Jane left the flat to wander the streets. As usual Belinda's head was fixed to her fingers, so that she could conduct a conversation should she wish to.

'So, Belinda, today we're going to the Black Church,' she announced quietly, crossing the street towards St Mary's Place.

She had decided to make the trip having heard Mrs Anderson in the room above theirs talking to Ma the previous week about that church and how if you walked three times anti-clockwise around it at midnight you could summon the Devil. Why anyone would want to summon the Devil at midnight or any other time was beyond her, but Ann Jane did not fear this entity because Ma had laughed softly at the notion and, later that day when Ann Jane had enquired, Da had told her the only devils were the ones with flesh and blood who'd take the last crumb from a person's mouth if they could. Vicious scroungers like Mr Murphy and the like who opposed working men joining the union.

Nevertheless the idea amused her. Because it was Easter Sunday, and therefore a very holy day, she decided to walk three times around the Black Church bearing in mind that it was not midnight. When she had done it she would certainly inform Mrs Anderson at the first opportunity. She crossed the street, glanced up at the church at the same time as she whispered in Belinda's pinkish left ear. What she whispered were not actual words, so much as half-formed lisps of intimacy and apprehension. She wanted to convince Belinda that this was an adventure worth having and that they would walk three times around and taunt the Devil, who could not appear even if he wanted to, because it was not midnight.

The church loomed sinisterly ahead, spikey-pinnacled and dark against the clear sky.

'So, Belinda, are you ready?'

Belinda's head nodded in response. The entire street was deserted. In the distance Ann Jane could hear the sounds of horses pulling carts, then the rumbling cartwheels themselves describing the passage of the afternoon. She also heard the shouts and cries of children. Some people had lit their fires, and already the air was trailing smoke with a grey-flannel haze hovering over certain buildings. But the sky was like a jewel and the day sunny. The Devil could never appear to anyone at such times. He represented darkness, fire and brimstone and the things the priests spoke of up at St Francis Xavier.

Ann Jane clutched Belinda to her chest as she planted her foot firmly to the right of the church door. She glanced once more over her shoulder and, as she sucked her small mouth in tight at the sight of the tall oval of the entrance, dimples appeared on her cheeks. She continued purposefully around the side of the church at an unvarying pace. When she had completed three circles of the building she stopped exactly where she had begun.

'Now, Belinda. Let's wait.'

Ann Jane regarded the high entrance, the arch and spike and interleaved stone that cradled the doorway. If he was going to appear it would be like a fizz of smoke or mist.

He would not descend from the archway. He would arise from below, moiling his way into her vision so that she would sense him even before she saw him, swirling up from beneath the dungeon-like cellar grid at the base of the church walls. She waited, feeling more satisfied by the second, as the moment expanded and there was no defining darkness, no spectre to obliterate her and the city around her.

'See Belinda?' She turned Belinda's face towards her own. 'Told you, didn't I? Nothing to worry about! Now we must go home because Ma will be wondering where we are.'

Ann Jane woke on Easter Monday to another bright day. Da had already left. Although he could not go to the races at Fairyhouse he wanted to be on the streets, to catch all the gossip as word came of winning horses. Ma did not get up at all, but clung to the Ba and stayed in the horsehair bed behind the dark green curtain that divided the room at night. Ann Jane could hear the Ba gurgling and snuffling. Her cold had become a thick and musical cough, like pipes playing out of tune as her small chest attempted to breathe.

Ann Jane moved quietly from her own tumbled bedding on the floor. Her brothers lay in deepest sleep. Jimmy's mouth was wide open and a trail of saliva drooled onto the flour sacking beneath his head. Seán and Tomás were silent, their chests rising and falling gently. Seán's browny fists, his black little fingernails, gripped the two woollen blankets that covered his body, as if in sleep he had to be on his guard.

She would go to Mrs Anderson and see if she was up. Perhaps she would have a slice of bread or some tea. She pressed hard at the skirt of her dress, as if to smooth out the creases, before pulling at her hair so that it was not hanging over her eyes. Grownups disliked hair falling into eyes and across noses. They had a habit of pushing it back, and not always gently, so that they could see you. Then they would study you as if there was something written in your eyes worth reading. Mrs Anderson was like that.

But Mrs Anderson was not up or else she had gone out. It was a quarter to twelve, almost midday. Just as Ann Jane was making her way down the long stairs, she heard a sound. It was not the usual creaks and dull thuds that were part of the acoustics of the big house in which the different families lived. There was no tin-whistle to be heard from the O'Flaherty's, nor was it the deep voice of Mr Toolan as he clobbered his wife; nor was it the secret silence— in itself a sound—that enveloped the floor on which the young Mr and Mrs Harry Dunne lived when they closed their door and shut out the world. So far, they had no childer, and Ann Jane knew they were happy, even though she had heard Mrs Anderson once remark that it was high time they had a little one to look after to take them down out of the clouds. On the one occasion she had glimpsed inside their tidy little room, there were no clouds to be seen, nor buffeting out from between the cracks in their door. The sound did not emanate from any of the usual sources. She looked around her. Above, the ceiling plaster was crumbling, the coving also breaking up with dampness. It was a sound from outside their world, one that she could not quite define, because it was not properly within her hearing so much as in her sense of something about to happen. It was a warning, she decided.

Out on the street, with Belinda on her fingers, she wandered to the bottom of North Great George's Street, turned right along Great Britain Street and found herself at the top of Sackville Street. From where she stood there was a new busyness and tension in the air which made her stop in her tracks. Her eyes were drawn to the one building that stood like a fortress on the street, the place Ma had told her to avoid at night because of the women who hung around beneath the portico. Around the GPO people were clustered in groups, heads moving intently as they turned to one another. Crowds milled further out on the street, gazing at the portico of the building as if something unusual was occurring. People were running. She whirled her head around. From behind, a group of lancers on horses proceeded steadily down the street in the direction of the post office. She pressed her body against the wooden frame of a shop doorway and shrank back as the men then charged until they drew level with the GPO. Ann Jane's hands flew to her ears as the guns fired and split the air. Belinda fell to the ground. Ann Jane dropped to her knees and quickly scooped up her doll again. Almost as quickly the horsemen galloped back up the street, the people shouting after them. A woman screamed. Not so far from where she stood someone cursed. Her entire body trembled, her heart like a struck anvil, relentless in her chest as she peered around the doorway again.

'Ah Jaysus, he's down!' someone called out.

At this, she sank to her knees and hunched up very small. Something terrible was happening. It was the Devil's revenge, for not being called at midnight, for having been fooled with in the middle of an Easter Sunday, God's holiest day. Ann Jane did not know how long she stayed there, watching from her position close to the ground. All she knew was that the sun had almost disappeared and the street lights had begun to glimmer. What was she waiting for when Hell seemed to be rising around them on the streets? Clutching Belinda tightly to her chest she lisped and whispered, soothing herself as the *pop-pop-pop!* she'd heard not so long ago from Mr Morosini's shop again filled the air. There would be fire, she knew, and brimstone, which was apparently worse, and instead of dolls' heads popping there would be devilish attempts to take the humans away from their innocent days with their hungry bellies. *Pop-pop-pop-pop!* She listened again and crouched on her hunkers for a long time. When it was completely dark she was still there with Belinda. She felt quite cold. The Devil himself had descended in their midst and it was entirely her fault. Because she had walked anti-clockwise around the Black Church, he had come up from Hell to possess the biggest building on Sackville Street, had driven the men and women in uniforms to rush inside and smash everything and the whole place would soon be blazing with demons.

But then she stirred. Her eyes tried to focus. Could it be? She snapped her eyes shut, as one of Mr Morosini's dolls might do, in case what she saw was not real, then as quickly snapped them open. It *was* real. Slowly she pushed herself to her feet, shaking her right foot which had gone numb. There was Mrs Anderson pushing a pram towards the conflagration, face flushed and happy. How peculiar, Ann Jane thought, to be pushing an empty pram so happily down the street, when Mrs Anderson's children were all grown and surely the shops were closed and there would be broken glass every place. But Mrs Anderson had spotted her and paused, holding the pram with one hand and placing the other on her hip. She was still wearing her everyday apron, although a red felt hat was perched jauntily on her head.

'Child! *What* are you doing here?'

Ann Jane shook her head, as if warning Mrs Anderson to stay away. There was too much danger.

'Child, do you hear me? What are you doing, Ann Jane Gleeson, when the city is in uproar? Are you light-headed?'

She was light-headed. How correctly Mrs Anderson had observed that. She was light-headed with fear, not hunger. The woman approached her then, pulling the pram behind her and stuck out her left hand in Ann Jane's direction.

'You'd be better off with me, my angel,' she said firmly, catching the child by the elbow and drawing her towards her.

Ann Jane did not resist. Perhaps Mrs Anderson was right. Perhaps the thing to do was to walk alongside her as she made her way bravely down the street in the darkness of the night with a pram. She might even pretend to be Mrs Anderson's daughter and she would be safe.

They approached a shop window in which the glass had been smashed and splintered. People crowded in, stepping over one another, jostling and pushing such was the rush. There was bread, criss-crossed and plaited, and bursting, shiny-crusted loaves scored with a knife, and there were cakes and sweets, and more chocolate than Ann Jane could ever have imagined as they followed the crowd inside. There was no fire or brimstone, merely glass to be avoided, and at last, fresh, sweet offerings on an altar of plenty.

'There you are, child. Sure don't you like fairy cakes too? Of course you do, of course you do ...'

Miss Moffat
Goes to Town

Éilís Ní Dhuibhne

'I'll cut the bollocks off your mother.'

The voice is a man's. It's loud. It's angry.

Miss Moffat hears a lot of interesting mobile phone conversations on this bus. For example, just the day before
yesterday, a young man—nice-looking, neatly dressed,
obviously on his way home from work—asked someone
'So do you want that pony?' Pony? The word intrigued
her. A slang word for some sort of drug, Miss Moffat had
a feeling that it might be. But she wasn't sure. She considered the possibility that he was referring to an actual horse.
'I'll see you beside the garage at eight,' had been his next
line. You could have a horse beside a garage, or even in a
garage, out in the western suburbs to which this bus would

eventually find its way. Pony could be a little horse, or some sort of drug. The transaction was of dubious legality in either case.

The voice of this man, today's man, is so angry that she is afraid to look too closely at him. Crazy people don't appreciate being looked at, even though they seem to be going out of their way to invite stares. She saw him getting on the bus, though, and waiting to pay his fare, or more likely show his free pass, to the driver. You could hardly fail to see him. He is dressed all in black—black hoodie, black jogging pants, one black shoe. He has only one foot. His right leg stops at the knee. Something about the way he is dressed suggests that it has been cut off, and not by a doctor and not long ago. The bottom of his trouser is wrapped around the place where the short leg ends; it looks like something packed in a shopping bag. Under his oxters, two big crutches. Before he made his threat, to somebody's mother, or to her mother, or maybe to everybody's mother, she felt sorry for him. But now she mainly feels frightened.

He comes down the aisle, repeating his threat, and sits down beside her. Not exactly beside, but just across the aisle. Nevertheless, he's very close. Just two feet separate them. And she doesn't like the look of those crutches. While he was walking—hobbling—they inspired pity. Now, when he's sitting down, with the crutches sort of resting in his lap, they look like weapons. Don't be silly! He can't do much harm, him and his one leg. No. The thing is, standing, he can't do much harm. But from his seated position wouldn't it be easy to pick up a crutch and hit someone with it? The nearest person to him, for example, who happens to be Miss Moffat herself.

'I'll cut the bollocks off your fucking mother!'

This is the third time he's expressed this rather strange intention, since Miss Moffat's mother, even if she happened to be alive, which she is not, had never had bollocks. Could it be that he's mixing up the word 'bollocks' with something else, breasts, for instance? Boobs would probably be the word he'd use, but that word sounds too harmless and comical to convey his message.

Who knows what he's talking about? The language of this part of the city is still foreign to Miss Moffat. 'Bollocks' might have more than one meaning, over here, on the northside? Miss Moffat is used to hearing words for sexual organs bandied about by angry men on some of the dodgier streets in the inner city. The words of choice refer to female organs (although not boobs). Anyway, now it's not so much 'bollocks' as the word 'cut' that bothers Miss Moffat.

She makes a snap decision. Get off the fucking bus. (See. She's picking up the local dialect without even trying. The language that surrounds you infects you.) There's another one right behind her, so she could hop on that. No time lost. She'll have to pay again. But her life is worth two euro fifteen cents.

She's on her way into town to her lesson in Russian. Just after she retired, Miss Moffat started taking extramural classes in Trinity College, the subject chosen because she likes Russian writers, by which she means Chekhov and Tolstoy. Turgenev. (If there are any Russian writers who haven't been dead for over a hundred years, she hasn't heard of them.) Into her second year of study there is no possibility of reading these writers in the original and she doubts that she ever will. So far, all she can manage are the short pieces in the textbook, about somebody buying a hat in a hat-shop—not a thing she has ever actually done, but maybe they still have hat-shops in Russia— or going to the doctor, or checking into a hotel. Miss Moffat can ask a Russian stall holder in the bazaar for a kilogram of apples or potatoes. How much does that cost? Thank you. Goodbye. And she can do some complicated negative interrogative sentences involving lots of finicky little particles which need to be placed in the correct order, for instance: Will you not put on your new hat tomorrow? But she hasn't got much farther than that. It is a difficult language and she tends to forget things. A year ago she knew how to get out of bed and wash herself and get dressed, but they have moved on to another textbook. It is almost two years since she encountered knives and forks, plates and cups. Now it is about flying from Moscow to Madrid for a conference about the internet. There is a lot of stuff about social media. You start off in the kitchen, bedroom and bathroom, as in life, but then you move on to the internet and conferences. The words go in one ear and out the other. Miss Moffat toddles along, scattering Russian words, long and short, to the wind.

To get anywhere, it would be necessary to go to Russia for a month or two, live with a family, immerse herself in the language. Miss Moffat doesn't think she is brave enough to face a Russian family for two months, or even two weeks, much as she desires variety and believes herself to be a good traveller. She has recently moved from the south to the northside of Dublin, for instance. It is a journey which very few people make in their lives. Migration is generally in the opposite direction. On good days she feels brave, and on bad days, foolhardy.

They come across the word for criminal in class today. *Prestupnik*. The teacher explained that it is based on the word *stup*, meaning step. (Good. Easy to remember then. Some of them are like English words or French words, though most are not.) A criminal is someone who oversteps the mark, who goes too far.

'What a brilliant word!' says Miss Moffat.

Of course it's written in the Cyrillic alphabet, in which all words look more important. **Престъпник.**

She seizes the opportunity to tell the class she met a criminal on the bus, on her way into town. Short digressions are permitted, ideally in Russian, in the interests of conversation practice.

'He was on something, I suppose,' she says this in English. Dublin seems to be full of men on something these days, she adds. Men who are full of anger, and shout about it to the world at large.

The teacher asks her to explain what 'on something' means. His English is excellent but he doesn't know all the idioms. Then he suggests a few ways of saying 'addicted' and 'drugged', in Russian. He agrees that there are a lot of loud and aggressive men in Dublin. It is almost as bad as Moscow, in that respect, and that surprised him when he first came because the other cities he knows, New York for instance, are much quieter. But he disagrees that the man on the bus was a criminal. The real criminals don't shout at random people on the bus. They keep a low profile.

This makes sense, Miss Moffat agrees, although privately she wonders. Maybe that's the way things work in Moscow and New York but around where she lives she's not so sure. The dodgy types she meets on Dorset Street seem proud of their lawlessness. They flaunt their aggression, like the heroes in ancient myths. Look at me, I'm stronger than you, I could kill you if I felt like it, they seem to proclaim, as they swagger along the street in gangs, or glower at her from derelict shop doorways. And anyway, how did that guy lose his leg from below the knee? She watches Netflix. She knows what the gangsters get up to, how they deal with people who can't pay for their drugs.

Miss Moffat plans to walk home after her Russian lesson but when she comes out it's raining, so it's back on the bus. On Upper O'Connell Street, through the window, she sees a man grabbing a woman. Oh, roughly he grabs her. The woman is young, a girl, and she's cycling on the wide footpath. The man grasps her shoulders and shakes her. Even though what he's saying is not audible from the bus it's easy to translate his body language. He's objecting to the girl cycling on the path. He's shouting, 'What the fuck do you think you're doing? Who the fuck do you think you are?' (Every second word is 'fuck' at this end of the street. Their vocabulary is quite limited.) He—the man, on the path—is pointing at the bicycle. After a while he shakes his head angrily and stalks off, in a huff. He's a short man with black hair and a bird face, with a black moustache. A black T-shirt. He thrusts his head forward, like an angry bull, as he strides down the pavement.

The scene is a bit like cartoons without words presented in the textbook. The student is asked to write the dialogue. These cartoons generally depict someone buying vegetables (or a hat), or catching a train. They don't involve *prestupniks*. Even if there are a lot of angry men on the streets of Moscow, out of their mind on heroin and shouting and swearing, they don't make their way into textbooks called *Russian for Foreigners* Book A2.

The girl gets back up on her bike and cycles on. There are not very many pedestrians on the path, the street is thick with traffic, buses and cars and trucks. No cycle lane. In Dublin, you are not allowed to cycle on the pavement—it's not like other European cities. The angry man had the law on his side. But what the girl was doing made sense, if her aim was not to get run down by a bus or a truck. And it's not legal to grab people by the shoulders and shake them either.

On the bus, someone starts to sing. It's a female voice, soft and tuneful, and she's singing in a foreign language. Not one Miss Moffat can name. She sings and sings. Miss Moffat is too polite to turn around and look—she wonders if perhaps the language is Romanian, if it is a Romanian gypsy. On the DART, which she used to travel on when she lived on the southside, people occasionally got on and sang or played a melodeon and then went around with a hat, hoping to collect money from passengers.

But when the song is over the singer just passes down the aisle to get off the bus. She's a small well-dressed girl, better dressed, in Miss Moffat's opinion, than most of the young women on this bus. She can't quite put her finger on it but they all share a certain style which is subtly different from what you see on the other side of the river. Mostly they wear black leggings, and little jackets, leather or denim, or something similar. Their faces are smooth with makeup and they sometimes have thick black lines drawn around their eyes. But this girl is trim and pretty and has a proper, knee-length, winter coat—a lovely coat, navy wool, with velvet covered buttons and a velvet collar. She doesn't look like a drug addict or an alcoholic. She could be from Dun Laoghaire or Shankill, like Miss Moffat herself. She steps lightly off the bus and walks away in the rain. Will no one tell me what she sings? Her song was sweet, though, not plaintive at all. A song of joy, or simple pleasure.

As always, when Miss Moffat gets home, she turns off the alarm and turns on the radio. She sits down on a soft chair she keeps in the kitchen. The news. A man has been arrested suspected of murdering a twenty-seven-year-old woman in an apartment on Manx Road.

The next road to hers.

She wonders if the murderer is the man with one leg. Or the man who grabbed the cyclist by the shoulders and shouted at her. The details of the case will gradually emerge. She'll find out on the nine o'clock news and if it is the man with one leg it will be big news.

The chances are that it is neither of those men, the ones she has encountered recently, those oversteppers of the mark. Her mark anyway.

But goodness knows.

It could be any of them really.

But the victim could not be the girl who sang the song, the girl in the blue coat with the velvet collar. Not her. Not a girl with a voice like that, and a coat like that.

Emigrant

Mirsad Ibišević

Edin watched the house in horror.

It had been a house of love, where his mother had called him her sunshine. It was where he had played with his younger sister. Where he had sat on the porch steps as a child, waiting for his father to return home from work. Sometimes his father would bring home treats. Ki-Ki caramel, which he and his sister loved.

Edin watched in disbelief as the house burned before him. Inside, his parents and his sister lay dead.

Why did I run away? Why didn't I let them kill me too?

Edin lay in the woods all night, watching, while everything he knew was destroyed.

Before dawn, he set off, bewildered. He didn't know where to go.

'Stop! Who is there?'

Edin lay on a hillside overlooking the road. He crawled to the edge of a rock and looked down. He saw a group of soldiers with blue helmets. There were rifles pointed in his direction, concealed by a truck.

'Come down. Don't worry. We are peacekeepers. UN.'

Edin raised his hands and stumbled onto the road.

'What's happened? You look terrified.'

'What are you doing on your own?'

Half an hour later Edin sat next to the truck, saying nothing. One of the soldiers got up and approached Edin, shaken by what he had heard. He wiped his eyes and embraced Edin as if he had met someone close to him, someone dear whom he had not seen for a long time.

'Try not to worry. You are safe now. My name is David. I am from Ireland. I have a brother your age back home.'

Edin liked Ireland. He even became accustomed to the rain and the cold. He didn't socialize too often, though, or make friends with the people he met. It wasn't that he didn't want to. He just didn't have the strength and he found it hard to trust other people.

He preferred to be on his own, in his small room on the North Circular Road. He liked to walk into the city, to the river, to sit on a bench and look at the water. It calmed him. He also liked to look at his watch. It was the only thing he owned that had survived the journey from Bosnia.

Edin got work washing dishes in a restaurant. The work wasn't difficult, and the people he worked with were kind. He was often struck by the differences in the worlds that he had come to know. Dublin, where people seemed to live lives of plenty and ease; and back home, where his family were dead, and where people had to struggle to get by.

He knew he could do more.

As more refugees arrived from Bosnia and from Croatia, Edin thought about using his experiences to become a translator. He made some inquiries and he was invited to take an exam. One morning, Edin was awakened by the sound of the letterbox. He rarely received post but now there was a brown envelope on the floor addressed to him. It was a letter from the Department of Immigration, offering him a job.

Edin was excited and nervous. He soon learned about his responsibilities, translating case files, and he was introduced to some of his colleagues in the department. He also met the woman he would work with and report to; her name was Fiona.

Edin thought Fiona was beautiful but reserved; he quickly realized she was extremely hard working. Fiona liked case files to be on her desk as soon as she arrived at the office. She didn't care how many files Edin had, or how much work each file entailed. They needed to be ready for her to process first thing in the morning. Edin struggled to translate all the documents in time, so he started taking work home at night. Edin worked harder and harder, and he found himself getting more and more tired. Eventually, he made the decision to confront Fiona.

'Listen, I can't do this anymore,' he said one morning, exhausted, having entered her office empty handed. 'I'm not a robot.'

Fiona looked at him in astonishment.

'Ok, let's talk. But not now.'

'When then?'

'After work. In the Porterhouse.'

That night Fiona and Edin talked. They barely mentioned work and for the first time, in a long time, Edin found himself relaxing in someone else's company.

Fiona lived in Ballyfermot, with her father and her mother. She was their only child and her father was very protective of her. As far as he was concerned, his daughter was the most precious thing in the world and her job was her ticket to a better life. He liked to know where she was, whom she was with, and when she would be home. Recently, she didn't always come home straight after work.

'This can't go on,' he announced one night at the dinner table. 'Where the hell do you go every night? What are you doing? What about your job?'

Fiona looked up.

'Dad, I'm a grown woman. I have my own life to—'

'To what?'

Before Fiona could finish, her father banged the table and stormed out of the room. Fiona turned to her mother, who already knew about Edin.

'Just give him time, pet.'

Fiona's father had to find out what his daughter was doing. Was she seeing someone? If so, who? What was he like? What did he do? What were his prospects?

The following day, her father went into the city centre and waited near St Stephen's Green, hoping to see Fiona after work. When he saw Edin and Fiona walking down the street together he jumped out in front of them.

'So that's your fella, eh!'

'Dad, what are you—'

'Hello, my name is Edin—'

'Aydin, eh? Where are you from? You're not Irish.'

'I am from Bosnia—'

Fiona's father exploded. 'Bosnia? What the ... Get your hands off my daughter!'

'Let him go, Dad. Edin hasn't done anything wrong. You can't stop—'

'What do you mean he hasn't done anything ... I don't want a stranger ... What do you know about him? Nothing. Maybe he's a murderer, or a criminal, or something. Stay away, Aydin, I'm warning you. If you know what's good for you.'

Fiona's father marched away, gesticulating angrily.

Fiona and Edin fell in love, despite Fiona's father's objections and prejudices. One weekend, Edin phoned Fiona and asked her if someone he knew—a man called Peter— could join them for a drink that night.

Fiona was surprised, as she'd never heard of anyone called Peter before. Indeed, Fiona had never met anyone Edin knew outside of work. She was curious and they agreed to meet later that evening in Temple Bar.

'Peter, this isn't easy ... I don't know where to begin ...' Edin explained that night. 'If your brother hadn't been there for me, who knows if I'd still be alive. David spent months going through embassies, the Red Cross, the UN, to transfer me here. Eventually he found someone who could add my name to a list of people who were being evacuated, people who were wounded and who were being sent to Dublin for treatment. I was listed as the brother of one of the wounded.'

'I will never forget the day they put us on a UN truck in Sarajevo. We headed through the city towards the airport. Burned-out cars. Destroyed buildings. Broken trams. Snipers. Explosions. I peeked through the window and I couldn't believe it. My ears were buzzing. I felt faint ...'

'When we were stopped at a Serbian checkpoint at the airport, I started to shake and sweat ... I couldn't breathe ... I nearly threw up ... I remember the terminal was full of sandbags and soldiers, and a plane was waiting on the runway. David was standing beside it.'

Edin paused. Fiona and Peter were silent. They didn't know where to look.

'David came up to me and held me tight. "We made it, Edy," he said. Edy. That's what he called me.'

Edin took off his watch and put it in front of Peter.

'Your brother gave me this. "Edy, listen to me," he said. "You go there and create a life for yourself. Peter will look out for you if you let him. He knows about you. He can't find happiness for you, though. You must do that for yourself. Take this watch and wear it for me. Wear it until you find happiness. When you do, give it to Peter, and tell him that I love him—".'

He placed the watch in Peter's hand.

'Take it. I don't need it anymore.'

Edin looked at Fiona and smiled.

Cíocras ('Relentless')

Caitlín Nic Íomhair

Tá siolla na cinniúna ag guairdeall ar bhruach mo bheola agus gach uile bhall, gach uile chill ionam ag impí orm gan scaoileadh leis. Tá sé ag amharc anuas orm, a chuid súl sáite ionam, a leathlámh ar mo chom, agus ní ag dul i bhfuaire atá sé leis an mhoill.

De nádúr an *affair* go mbíonn an chumarsáid gonta, srianta, patuar fiú.

Árasán @9
Brady's an8
Croí isteach
Slán abhaile

Ní theastaíonn aon *paper trail* uaidh, ná ní maith leis cur isteach ar *family time*. Rug sí air—a bhean—uair agus iad ar sciuird go Ikea, é ag breathnú ar a ghuthán gach re bomaite agus muid ag troid ar WhatsApp. Bhí obair aige bréag a chumadh ar an spota di, nó ba nós leis é féin a thumadh go hiomlán sa rud a bhí thart air, leabhragáin Billy go fiú. Ag coimhéad cluiche sacair a dúirt sé.

Seo baolach, Bla. Scairt an8.

Bhí an t-ádh orm an oiread sin féin a fháil, nó dhealraigh sé níos minice ná a athrach nár rith mé leis, nár smaoinigh sé orm ónar dhruid sé doras m'árasáin go dtí an chéad choinne eile, buidéal fíona i leathlámh agus bláthfhleasc *cheesy* faoina ascaill. Ba ríchuma liom faoi sin—bhí leannán eile agam, agus ní duine mé a bheadh gaibhte le téacsáil síoraí ar nós

—*Cad a bhí agat don bhricfeasta lol?xox*

—*Leite! Ium! xoxox*

Bí ann nó bí as, a deirimse, agus ní bhíonn srian ar bith air agus é anseo. Baineann sé lán na súl asam i dtólamh, ionas go dtig luisne ar mo ghrua nuair a scarann sé mo chosa le siúráil agus le saint. Nuair a bhíonn sé liom, bíonn sé liom, fiú muna mbíonn muid riamh os comhair an tsaoil.

Ní sárú rómhór, dar leis, a scinneadh gasta rialta ó chuing chúng an phósta, a fhad is a dhiúltaíonn sé cos a chur i dtaca, gan moilliú riamh i gcríocha drúisiúla mo cholainne. An dlíodóir ann, is dócha, ag meá ceart agus cóir, cion agus pionós. Rinne sé a chás go sollúnta nuair a thoisigh muid ag suirí, le gontacht a chuaigh i bhfeidhm orm. Gur mhóidigh sé os comhair an tsaoil gur thoiligh sé aonfheoil a dhéanamh le bean amháin agus gur sárú ar a mhóid a bheadh ann, dá mbeadh cuid agamsa de. Loighic shaofa, ar ndóigh, nuair a thug sé faoi achan ghníomh collaí eile le craos, ach ní hí An Bhean Eile a scríobhann gramadach an chaidrimh.

Bhí mise sásta le cuid ar bith de. Ní raibh aon ghá agam leis an roinnt chinniúnach—má bhí sí chomh cinniúnach sin.

Ba leor an pógadh. An chuimilt. An muirniú. An fáisceadh. An cuachadh. An chigilt seo, an siosarnach siúd. Gaoth an fhocail i mo chluas. A mheáchan leáite anuas orm. Teas a lámh ar mo chraiceann. Brú óna bhríste ar mo bholg. *Zip* mo chuid jeans á scaoileadh agus ruathar dána méire faoi bhanda coime an *lingerie*.

Ach anocht, anocht tá leathbhuidéal thar an ghnáth ólta aige agus tá an dlíodóir inmheánach ina chnap ólta. Anocht tá teas an tsamhraidh ag réabadh trína chorp agus tá athrú meoin tagtha air. Théis an tsaothair a chuir muid orainn féin gan géilleadh don chathú, théis a liachtaí sin oíche ar tharraing sé uaim ar an leaba seo. Níor ghéill muid, agus ba leor é, go dtí anocht.

Tá an soicind crochta ag imeacht ina bhomaite. Tosaím ag scaoileadh cnaipe a bhríste nuair a bhainim siar asam féin. Mo ghuthsa go cinnte, ach ar neamhchead iomlán uaim.

'Stop.'

Tránn an teas ón seomra. Tá iontas air, shílfeá, agus díomá. Baineann sé a leathlámh ó mo chom go grod. Iompaíonn sé ionas nach idir mo chosa atá sé níos mó ach in aice liom ar an leaba, gonta ag an diúltú, an dúil réabtha ag frustrachas agus cantal. Coiscim abairt chrosta i mo scornach. Ba é a riail óir mhallaithe féin é.

Triallaim ar an chistin, spalptha, le cúlú ón teannas. Ag méanfach, lasaim an raidió. Caint in áit ceoil— neamhghnách. An phaindéim, ar ndóigh ...

Ní fada go dtugaim liom éirim na cainte. *Lockdown.* Gan cead amach ag mac máthar nach oibrí éigeandála é i ndiaidh meán oíche anocht nó go bhfógrófar a mhalairt. Péas armtha ar an tsráid le ceadúnas a ghrinneadh. Tithe tábhairne bánaithe, carranna tréigthe ar bhóithre a bhfuil snaidhm rófhada tráchta orthu. Deimhniú ón Uachtarán go bhfuil cumhachtaí speisialta ceadaithe do na fórsaí slándála ó 00.01 ar aghaidh.

Tá a ghuthán ina thost ach lasann an scáileán achan re bomaite ag fógairt scairteanna caillte.

Amharcaim ar an am. Rómhall le *wifey* a bhaint amach roimh chuirfiú. *Shit.*

* * * * *

Uair an chloig níos déanaí, buidéal eile diúgtha, cruinníonn muid ár maoin le chéile. Cárta creidmheasa agus cárta dochair an duine, maille le cúpla gearrthóg páipéir agus uimhir orthu. Airgead na seanlaethanta. Airgead sna gutháin, leis, ach a cheannsan marbh. Amharcaim air, ag dealú boinn ó nótaí go deifreach agus ag comhaireamh faoina anáil, solas lasta sa tsíleáil os a chionn nár las mé féin riamh.

Thug muid iarraidh chiotach ar chodladh in aon leaba, an chéad oíche sin, ach b'fhuar againn é. Sceitimíní na héigeandála ormsa, agus buairt i bhfad níos bunúsaí air siúd: bhí cinnte air bréag inchreidte a chumadh in am agus ba chuma, ní raibh luchtaire Apple ar bith agam agus bhí cumhacht a iPhone tráite cheana ag a cuid glaonna siúd. Ní thiocfadh leis glaoch uirthi ó mo ghuthánsa, chreid sé. Masla thar mhaslaí a bheadh ansin. Agus ní raibh a huimhir de ghlanmheabhair aige cibé.

Bhí cúthaile agus ciotaíl ag baint leis an mhaidin dár gcionn, leis. An fear seo a shamhlaigh mé le sárú agus le spraoi go tobann ina aoi chun tí agam. Mé ag tindeáil tae air, ceann faoi orm faoi shalachar na cistine, leithscéalach nach raibh níos mó bia istigh agam. Scrúdaigh sé na leabhragáin, ghrinnigh sé na pictiúir theaghlaigh. Bhraith mé é sa mhullach orm, go raibh mo sháith agus tuilleadh agam den fhear seo nach mbíodh riamh ar fáil go hiomlán.

Oró 'sheanduine 'sheanduine pósta, oró 'sheanduine is mairg a phóg tú.

Bhí sé ina choda beaga ag seanphictiúr díom nuair a bhí folt fada fionn á fhás agam do Goldilocks. Rinne sé jóc nár thaitin liom, á rá go mbeadh mo ghrágán buí anois foirfe do bhuachaill bunscoile nó Boris Johnson. Thug mé faoi deara, fosta, mar a fhuaimníonn sé m'ainm: Blah-heen, i neamhchead don síneadh fada.

Thuig sé údar mo chantail sar i bhfad. Ní dhearna sé ach gáire socair, agus mo ghiall a iompú i dtreo a bheola le méara éadroma maithiúnacha. Bhí taithí aige ar dhlúithe, ar aontíos le bean. Ar anáil bhréan na maidine, ar stocaí faoin cheannadhairt, ar níochán *knickers*. Thosaigh sé ag magadh orm, do mo leanstan timpeall an árasáin mar a bheadh peata, mo shrónaíl, ag soncáil faoi m'easnacha, gan spás ar bith a thabhairt domh d'fhonn mo chantal a thabhairt chun buaice. Bhris an gáire orm agus thit muid de phleist ar an tolg ag pulcadh póg.

* * * * *

Seachnaím scairteanna Skype ar eagla go nochtfaidh sé os comhair an cheamara. Maím do chlann is cairde go bhfuil mé meath-thinn sa leaba. Ní thrustaim nach ndéanfaidh sé trup inteacht a chuirfeadh go tóin poill ar fad mé leofa siúd atá lárnach i mo shaol agus nach dtuigfidh, nach maithfidh seo go deo domh.

Tugann sé amach domh as a bheith ag osnaíl le mífhoighne agus mé ag ithe. As méanfach a dhéanamh agus muid ag coimhéad Netflix. As a bheith ag timireacht fríd an teach seachas ag cur tic le seicliosta. Nuair a léim an *Guardian* seasann sé taobh thiar díom, á léamh liom. Cloisim é ag feadaíl go meidhreach sa seomra folctha.

Agus mé ag prapáil dinnéir, airím uaim an béile ite go deifreach ón fhriochtán, i mo sheasamh ag an doirteal. An tuirse a bhraith mé ar éirí agus ar dhul a luí. An *commute* féin, an uair dhíomhaoin sin ar thraein. An saol díomhaoin.

Smaoiním ar a bhfuil caillte aige amuigh ansin, gan mhairg is cosúil. Smaoiním ar a bhean—ar a cuid feirge agus imní, ní foláir, ar a mearbhall. Nó a faoiseamh, b'fhéidir, ní fios. Smaoiním gur gar atá déanta agam di. Smaoiním gur seo an rud is *karma* ann: lán do bhéil is tuilleadh den rud nach raibh ceadaithe duit.

Smaoiním go mb'fhéidir go bhfuil an víreas orainn beirt, agus gur *karma* é go bhfaighimis bás brocach le chéile sa spás róchúng seo ar nós na n-ainniseoirí bochta ar leáigh *lava* orthu agus iad ag bualadh craicinn in Pompeii. Scéilín suarach a líonfaidh colún nuachta nuair a bheas seo uilig thart agus a bhainfidh gáire dóite as iar-chairde: 'cheating couple's corona conjugal concludes in calamity.'

* * * * *

Tá cíocras ann a scanraíonn mé agus a thaitníonn liom. Tá mo chuid fíona ar fad diúgtha aige, agus ansin chrom sé ar mo chuid raithní. Choinnigh sé greim an fhir bháite orm inár leaba aontumhach aréir, ionas nár bhraith mé an oíche ar fad ach teas marbhánta a cholainne brúite le mo thaobh do mo scaladh. Ransaigh sé fríd mo chuid leabhar ar fad gan foighde a bheith aige tabhairt faoi cheann ar bith acu a léamh i gceart. Dá dtabharfainn *quiz* dó anois ní thiocfadh leis teideal ná clúdach a thabhairt chun cuimhne.

Faighim suas le huair an chloig sa lá liom féin faoi uisce muirneach an fholcadáin ach thabharfainn an leabhar go gcluinim é taobh amuigh den doras ag fanacht, ag dréim le fuinneamh a shú asam athuair. An paisean ann a d'fhág i mo staic thíos faoi mé, a chuir drithlíní faoi mo ladhracha, a bhain searradh asam faoina mheáchan, tá faitíos orm anois go n-alpfaidh sé mé de theann leimhe, de theann leadráin, de theann na faic.

Ón uair nach bhfuil a dhath eile le déanamh, tarraingím anuas orm é agus cuirim mo mhéar i mbéal an alpaire.

Relentless
Caitlín Nic Íomhair

The decision is mine, but I have to make it *now*.

I feel my consent straining in my throat, prying my lips apart as the rest of me wills it back. He's looking down at me, hands on my hips, eyes boring into me, perhaps mistaking my hesitation for coquettish teasing. He's not for budging.

Part of playing away is keeping communications innocent, even terse, but never encoded enough to be incriminating:

Apartment @ 9
Brady's tonight
Best of luck today
Safe home

Even then, he doesn't like texting. He lives in fear of the paper trail—bank statements, errant hairs on his suit jacket, hotel pens or what have you—and he guards his 'family time' jealously. His wife confronted him once about being glued to his phone during a trip to Ikea. We were having a spat and, sensing that our relationship was the one most likely to implode that day, he kept fishing out his phone every two seconds to check his WhatsApp. This was highly suspect from a man whose best feature is the relentless focus he fixes to the task at hand, even if that's buying *Billy* bookcases for the spare room. Sudden inattention from him burns like a slap.

He had to build his own flat-pack excuse on the spot: a football match gone to sudden death.

Risky business, Blah. Call you tonight.

Somehow he managed to render into text exactly how he mispronounced my name just slightly every time, as though he'd had a very successful tongue graft but from a Dane or a Dutchman who just couldn't, on principle, yield to the exigencies of two entire síneadh fadas[1] in one name.

Much as that irked me, I'll admit I was quite honoured that'd he'd name me in a text. I often wondered if he even remembered me during those interludes between when he pulled the door shut behind him, and his next appearance with a bottle and a cheesy bouquet tucked under his oxter. Not that I was fussed either way; I wasn't quite 'single' myself and there's nothing I hate more than that constant, mind-numbing text chatter between co-dependent lovers:

—What did you have for breakfast lol?xox
—Porridge! Yum!Xoxox

Be here when you're here and be gone when you're gone. That's the only way if you ask me, and he seemed to fit the bill perfectly. He would pour his focus into me as soon as we met and be mine until he left. He could make me blush and squirm just by looking at me, and when he left I'd smarten up again.

A good job it was too, that intensity, since physically he was almost prudish. His logic, such as it was, went thus:

[1] Accent mark in the Irish language.

it wasn't totally unconscionable for him to regularly dash out beyond the Pale of his marriage as long as he didn't get too comfy out here in no-man's-land. He was just visiting, he felt he had to stress, not taking out a lease. Not planting trees. He had promised to fuse flesh with only one woman and he couldn't betray that by going all the way with me. Pretty warped stuff, if you ask me, since nothing else was off the table between the sheets, but the Other Woman doesn't write the rules of engagement.

He made his case almost solemnly when we first started dating—the lawyer in him, I suppose, tipping minuscule measurements of right and wrong into the scale to achieve a balance which let him have what he wanted and not feel guilty about it. He would happily pay in deprivation, but not in consequence.

He didn't seem to trust that it was fine by me. Drama and betrayal were not what attracted me to him. I'd take what he was willing to give and happily forgo that ultimate step, if sex somehow really was the be-all-and-end-all.

Anyway, the rest was plenty. The way his breath in my earlobe made me squirm under him, the heat of his hands on my skin, how his trousers poked at my belly button and the rush of surprise and relief when I felt his fingers finally pulling at my waistband.

Tonight, though, things are different. He's had a change of heart. Nothing to do with the extra half bottle of wine he drank, enough to knock out his internal lawman. Or that prickly wine-heat that practically undresses you itself, saying 'fuck it, we're animals and we're already sweating, might as well'.

He's still staring down at me. It started hot but now it's getting awkward. I've undone his belt and the zip is half down when I am interrupted by my own voice speaking unbidden.

'Stop.'

The fever breaks. I can tell he's surprised as he untangles himself from me and lies staring at the ceiling in silence. I'm not sure if he's hurt or just frustrated but his reaction irritates me. I swallow an angry reminder that these are his rules we're playing by.

The room reeks of anti-climax. I head for the kitchen, partly because I'm thirsty but mostly just to escape. I feel groggy, like when you wake up mid-dream. I turn on the radio but every station is all talk, no music.

It doesn't take long for me to get the gist. Lockdown. Curfew. No one allowed out after midnight tonight until told otherwise, essential workers excepted. Armed cops at checkpoints. Hospitals and supermarkets quickly drafting passes for staff who have to ignore every instinct and go outside where the virus lurks, malevolent and imperceptible. The pubs have been instructed to shut, traffic is said to be endless and some cars have even been abandoned on roads—by throngs of lovers rushing back to their 2.4 by midnight, who knows?

My lover's phone is on silent but the screen lights up every minute as the missed calls rack up. I check the time but I already know—too late for him to get back to wifey before curfew. Shit.

* * * * *

An hour and another bottle into lockdown, we decide to pool our resources—credit and debit cards, some folding money which seems completely defunct now, some savings and my pitiful stock in cryptocurrency. We fled to money first, as if we could somehow buy our way out of this. I watch him as he separates coins and notes, totting up the total under his breath, the Big Light which I have never lit shining down on him.

We sleep awkwardly that first night, my mind racing about the pandemic while he's preoccupied with a much more local concern—he hadn't come up with a convincing lie in time, and it was moot now anyway. His phone had died after the millionth missed call and I don't have an Apple charger. I told him to use my phone but he refused, saying it would be an insult to her. Plus he didn't know her number off by heart.

We were still awkward and shy the next morning, in fact. I felt more like a hostess than a lover, making him cups of tea and apologizing for the mess. We normally spent our dates chilling in the bedroom but I was beginning to feel like I should ask him to sign the guest book on his way out.

That's if he'd ever leave. No more short shocks and thrills. Desire had no chance to rebuild, anticipation had flipped entirely into looking forward to being alone. We'd skipped carnal knowledge for something much more revealing.

He pored over my books and examined my family photos, all while standing so close to me that I could feel his breath on my neck. He found out 'Bláithín' means 'little flower' and started calling me 'flower' in a Cockney accent. He made countless stupid jokes and admired the wrong things about my belongings. He said I have an air of Boris Johnson until I comb my mop in the morning. I know he was going for levity, not trying to hurt me.

He soon understood why I was short and distant. He didn't bite back, just laughed gently and drew me to his lips with indulgent fingers. Intimacy was his default, after all, all morning breath and irritating idiosyncrasies and knickers drying on radiators. He started acting the lig,[2] following me around the apartment giving me no room, sniffing at me and poking me in the ribs, trying to get a reaction. Eventually it worked and my exasperation

---

[2] Behaving like an idiot.

turned to laughter. We threw ourselves onto the sofa and kissed till we got giddy.

I can't quite shake the feeling that we both have the virus already, that karma will do its thing and we'll die sordid and cramped little deaths together like those poor sods in Pompeii whose interrupted O faces are preserved forever in volcanic rock. I imagine ex-friends relishing the sheer humiliation of it all, relieved the headlines were not about them: cheating couple's corona conjugal concludes in calamity.

I avoid Skype because I don't trust him to leave me alone long enough to get through a call. I tell friends and family that I'm in bed, poorly. All he'd have to do is chirp up an answer during a Zoom quiz and I'd be sunk, shunned by people who know I know better.

* * * * *

I'm clearly getting on his nerves, too. He tells me off for sighing impatiently while I eat, for yawning through a Netflix box set. I potter about at the housework when I should be methodical, apparently. When I read the *Guardian*, he stands behind me and reads along with me, occasionally sucking his teeth at what he's reading. He whistles every time he goes to the toilet.

I miss eating food out of the pan, stood at the sink, no fuss or candles. I miss feeling wrung out by the day.

Even the commute, when idle time seemed precious and indulgent, not stultifying. I miss being single.

I can't help but think about what he's lost out there, seemingly without much concern. I think of his wife. How baffled she must be, and angry, and worried. Or simply relieved. Maybe I did her a favour. Maybe this is karma, being stuck in an All You Can Eat with no appetite.

* * * * *

He has a relentlessness about him that goes far beyond mere appetite, a compulsion that doesn't seem to bring him any joy. It almost feels violent at times, but when it's me that's on the menu it is flattering and hot as hell. The rest of the time he just hoovers up whatever else is in the room without a by-your-leave or a 'do you want half?' First he finished off the wine, then set about my dope like he couldn't rest till he had exhausted all opportunities for distraction. He's gone through all my books without actually stopping to finish a single one. He held on to me so tight last night in our sinless bed that his heat, scalding and damp, felt like a symptom.

I get up to one entire hour to myself each day in the comfort and privacy of a bath, but I swear even with my head underwater and the sound distorted I can hear him panting at the door, waiting to demand his share of whatever energy I have recouped. He expects me to have something new to give—news? from the bathroom?—and his disappointment makes me feel inadequate and unappealing, like stale fast food or daytime tv. His passion used to possess me, make my toes curl and my back arch under his weight. Now it kind of scares me, like when he's fingered every hardback spine and gobbled up any morsel of amusement in the gaff, I'll be next. And not out of love, either, but compulsion, or boredom, or lack of a better option.

And since I too have nothing else to do for the foreseeable, I pull him down on top of me and slip a finger between his snapping jaws.

Arrival

Melatu Uche Okorie

She emerged from the baggage collection area in the arrivals hall and sat on her suitcase. Rustling through her handbag and unable to locate her hairbrush, she stood up and finger-brushed her weave, after which she strengthened her tight-fitting denim-on-denim outfit. Remembering she had to keep an eye out for the person who was to collect her, she looked up and encountered a man's stare, as if he had been willing her to look up for a long time.

It was a small airport, and he was standing a few feet away at the waiting area. He smiled, and when she returned his smile, he walked confidently towards her. She watched him strolling over, deciding he must be the one asked to collect her.

She ran her eyes over him. He did not fit the image of a taxi driver. He was nicely dressed. The only thing Udeme had given her as a description for the person was that he was tall. He hugged her when he reached her. It was quick and unexpected. She smiled courteously. He took hold of her suitcase as if she was an old friend and she removed her hand from the handle. Before she could ask if he was the one sent, he turned and headed for the airport's large sliding doors, wheeling her suitcase beside him. Hanging her handbag over her shoulder, she hurried after him.

'Is that all you came with?' he asked, when she reached his side.

'Yes,' she said, smiling and nodding politely.

'I've never seen a woman in my life travelling with one suitcase.'

She tutted and shook her head. Of all the issues in the world to choose, he had to pick the one topic that would rile her. 'Every woman is different,' she said, giving him a scolding glance.

'So they say.' His answer was so offhanded it could only be an unconscious thought said aloud.

'Hey,' she snapped, smacking his nearest arm. Her eyes met his surprised look. 'Sorry,' she added, putting out a hand apologetically.

He laughed, turning away, shrugging and nodding all at once as if to say he probably deserved the smack.

He stopped beside a shiny, white, BMW, which, like his looks, was not what she was expecting. She tried to steal a glance at him from under her lashes. He caught her eye, returning it with a steady look of his own. When he dropped his gaze, he rummaged in his pockets and brought out his car keys. Unlocking the car door for her first, he took her luggage to the boot. She settled into the front passenger's seat and, as she waited for him to get into the car, her mind flew to what awaited her at the end of the journey. Instantly, she felt a tightening in her lower abdomen.

She heard the slam of the boot and soon after, he settled into the car. Putting on his seatbelt, he turned to her. 'I'm Paddy, by the way.' Opening a compartment in the car, he took out a business card.

Nodding to acknowledge his name, she took the card from his hand. 'Grace,' she said, looking at the names on his business card: Patrick Paddy McGuinley.

'Graaace?' he asked. Something in his voice made her look at him and she saw that he was looking at her strangely. 'Was that the name your woman gave me?' he mumbled, the question directed more to himself than to her. Pinning her with a stare, as if she would escape if he dropped his eyes, he tapped his breast shirt pocket, and ascertaining that whatever he was looking for was in there, he dipped two fingers into the pocket and took out a folded piece of white paper. Hesitantly, he read out of the paper, 'KA—C-H—I.'

Grace gestured for the paper. He handed it to her. She recognized the handwriting as Udeme's, the scrawl similar to those on the parcels he sent her from time to time.

Grace turned the paper in her hand. She had heard of how *Oyinbos* were distrustful of Nigerians, how every word from a Nigerian was dissected and examined. She wondered if this was going to be one such occasion and braced herself. After a minute or two, when he still did not say a word, it occurred to her that he may never ask her directly what she was guessing he wanted her to confirm.

Grace held up the piece of paper and read the letters one after the other—'K-A-C-H-I, KAA-CHI,' she said, correcting his earlier pronunciation of her name. Turning to see if by pronouncing her name right she had managed to convince him that she was Kachi, she saw that he looked preoccupied. Holding out the paper in a such a way that he could see it too, Grace said, 'You see, in Igbo language, our *K-A* is the same as the English *C-A*.'

'But it is you?' he asked, his tone his way of telling her that he couldn't care less.

She smiled to herself. Her emphasis on how to pronounce Kachi had been intentional, to get under his skin. Did he really think she would have got into his car if she doubted that he was the one Udeme said was going to pick her up from the airport? As if she had never seen a BMW before! Handing the paper back to him, she explained, 'Oh, that is me. Kachi is my Igbo name. My English name is Grace. I told you Grace because I felt it would be easier for you to say and remember.'

'Oh yeah, Grace is definitely easy to remember,' he said. She glanced suspiciously at him. Was he being sarcastic? But his face was blank. A few seconds passed and he still made no move to start the car. She looked around her. The carpark was almost empty, and the road was free.

Wondering what more he needed from her to reassure him that she was Kachi, she said irritably, 'The person who sent you to collect me is Jessica. Her brother's name is Udeme. Jessica's son is, erm—what is it called—autistic. His name is …' Grace faltered. Should she even be giving him all this information about Udeme's family?

'Yeah, the little boy,' he said. 'You mean, erm …' he paused to start the car.

'Jason,' Grace supplied, relieved he knew Jason. Because she was watching him, she caught the smile that crossed his face.

'Ahh, yeah,' he said slowly, moving into the road.

Was his earlier pause intentional? Something about his lazy drawl told her Jason's name did not come to him when she said it. Did he want her to say Jason's name to check how well she knew the family? Why didn't he just ask her for her ID then? Wouldn't that be better than pretending he trusted she was who she said she was, yet doubting all her words? She would tell Udeme about this when she saw him. Grace tried to imagine his reaction, mentally going through their various phone conversations where she had told him of disagreements with other people. With a start, she realized he never said anything this way or that. It seemed her soon-to-be husband kept his thoughts mostly to himself.

Paddy stopped at the carpark exit machine and slotted in a card. The overhead barriers opened and as the car passed through, Grace resolved to say nothing throughout the journey. Looking inside her handbag for something to read and finding nothing, Grace crossed her arms and stared out the window to take in the scenery.

The city, from what she could see, was much smaller than Lagos, and the cars on the road even fewer than what one would find in a street in Lagos.

Driving clear of the airport, Paddy followed an overhead sign with DUBLIN written boldly on it. 'I'll be stopping at that garage real quick,' he said, jerking his head towards a petrol station in the distance.

Grace smiled politely, nodding. He turned on his indicator. A car in front of him indicated its intention to pull into the same petrol station. He followed the car in and parked behind it. Turning, he smiled at her. She smiled back briefly and turned away. In the car in front were a man and a woman with two small children in car seats. The children were seated facing the back window. The youngest held a feeding bottle to her mouth.

Paddy waved at them. They stared back at him unblinking. He laughed at their unimpressed stare and Grace hid a smile. The man in the car in front got out to put fuel in the car. He was wearing a plain pink T-shirt and blue jeans, with sandals. He waved at the children. They turned their heads from staring at Paddy and Grace to watching him as he held the fuel nozzle to their car.

In a few hours, Grace thought to herself, she would be starting her new life as Udeme's fiancé. In two days' time, she would meet Udeme for the first time in the flesh. He was on a five-day shift at the hospital where he worked; today was his third day. Grace wiped her palms on her jeans.

They had met on Facebook. He had seen her picture on his older sister Jessica's page and sent her a friendship request. Soon, they were inseparable—virtually. Two years of a long-term relationship and a proposal online. WhatsApp. Skype. Viber. Facebook Messenger. Daily video calls observing each other doing ordinary things. How much different would it be from now? Living together. Speaking face to face. Would it render the habits they had built over time meaningless?

What are you cooking today? Rice.

What did you eventually make yesterday? Yam and Stew.

What have you decided to wear? The blue shirt. The brown dress.

What time will you get home? Nine o'clock.

What time did you get in last night? Just past midnight.

If communication is what every relationship needed, they had done that plenty. If occasional fights and make-ups are signs of a strong relationship, then they have nothing to worry about, for even in their guarded communications, they managed to find things to argue about.

Why did you stay out that late?

You told me you were going alone but I saw the pictures you posted on Instagram. You were with friends!

She reached out a hand and rubbed her other arm gently just as the car in front of them drove away and Paddy pulled into the vacated space close to the petrol pump. Opening his door, one leg out of the car, he turned to her. 'Do you want anything?' jerking his head towards the shop attached to the petrol station. Grace shook her head. Smiling, he listed out things for her to consider: 'Water? Gum? Snacks?' as if he could sense she was annoyed with him, and he wanted to placate her. Grace shook her head at all the options.

He left the car and she watched him as he filled the tank. When he was done, he put his head through the car window. 'Are you sure you don't want a bathroom break?'

Laughing, Grace shook her head, pleading for him to stop. She saw him smile before he walked away towards the shop. Back on the road again, he asked if she would mind him turning on the radio. She shook her head.

'What kind of music do you like?' he asked, pressing a button on the car radio. 'This plays Country music,' he said, lifting his eyes enquiringly as the twang of a Country song filled the car. He pressed the button a few times. 'This one is Trad,' he paused briefly for her to hear a fast-paced fiddle tune. 'That's, erm, Irish folk music,' he explained, pressing the radio tuner furiously again. He found a Jazz station playing old Blues and stopped. 'This sounds alri',' he said, glancing at her. She nodded.

They sang the end of the song together, and when the next song came on, they continued to sing bits that they knew out loud.

'This is good,' Grace said to him, pointing to show she was referring to the radio station.

'Yeah, they're good,' he agreed, nodding slowly.

Leaning back on her seat, Grace tried to imagine herself with Udeme, listening to music just like she was doing with Paddy. With a frown she realized Udeme might not like the songs that were playing. The clips of music he sent to her were mostly new Afro beats, with videos of half-naked women shaking their bodies frantically. It made her reluctant to send him songs she liked, as they were slower, and were more about the words than the beat.

A question that had been bugging her since they left the airport came into her mind. Grace turned to Paddy. 'How did Jessica describe the person you are to pick?' she asked, watching him closely.

'God knows!' he said, shrugging. 'She told me an African woman, and I grabbed the first one I saw.'

Stunned at his nonchalance, Grace gave a loud laugh. He chuckled at her laugh.

'Could you imagine what would happen if I arrived with the wrong African woman?'

She swung round to face him, covering her mouth with her hand. 'Do you think something like that is possible?'

'Oh, God knows,' he said. Suddenly, he laughed and shook his head as if the image of what he had said had just played out in his mind.

Imagining it too, she started to laugh. Still smiling, she glanced at him, their eyes met and held. He turned his head slowly back to the road. Grace turned hers to her window, embarrassed.

As if he could sense a drop in her mood, he asked if she had any favourite Nigerian musician. She stayed with the question as if giving it some thought, as she had seen him do with everything he said, like he weighed his words.

'I don't really have any favourite. I think most of the greats have passed and the ones we have left are merely singers.' She looked at him to see if he understood and she saw that he was nodding his head.

'Do you like Fela Kuti?' he asked. She nodded, laughing. 'I have his CD somewhere in this car,' searching his glove compartment.

She made a smoking sign at him. 'You must be a fan then.'

'Ahh, sometimes.'

They chatted about this and that, and sometimes they just shared a comfortable silence, at which point one of them would either sing or hum to the music on the radio.

She relaxed into the comfort of her seat as they passed what looked like a town. 'So, it's straight to the Republic now, eh?' she asked.

'Oh, ye-ah,' he drawled, stretching the words. She smiled at the way he never said a simple yes or no, wondering if he was even aware of it.

'You know, I had always thought Ireland was part of Britain,' she said absentmindedly.

'No-o-oh.' He said the word in three syllables. 'We fought for our independence just like you guys. The British wanted to kill us off before then.'

'Really?' she asked, raising her head to check if he was joking.

'All true,' he said, nodding to show his seriousness. 'A few years ago, things were so bad everyone was emigrating. You would find lots of Irish people in Australia, America, England … I used to live in England myself.'

'Really?' she repeated, looking at him.

He smiled ruefully and nodded. 'I used to work for a charity that provided homes for men who left Ireland when they were young to work in England. A lot of them had lost touch with their families. Ye-a-h—there was a man we helped to bring to Ireland once. He had a sister living in Mayo.' He glanced at her to see if she knew the place. She shook her head gently, while gesturing for him to carry on with his story. 'They called him one day and told him his niece was getting married in Mayo. Ye-a-h, we encouraged him to go for the wedding. He agreed. We got him a ticket for the ferry and all that, and he got himself a suit and got ready, went all the way to Mayo, but he didn't enter the church. Just wouldn't go in. He had been a long time away and didn't know how people would receive him. He turned around and got the next bus to Dublin and got on the next ferry back. Could you believe that?'

'That's sad,' Grace said.

'There are many stories like that. They were just too embarrassed to return home.' He glanced at her and smiled self-deprecatingly. 'There are charities like that too for Caribbeans who came in the sixties to England.'

'I didn't know about all of that,' Grace said, looking at him with a new kind of respect.

'Ye-a-h, the world is full of stories, isn't it?'

Grace nodded, turning to look out of her window, a quietness settling over her. He stared at the road ahead.

When he spoke again, it was to tell her they were approaching the border. Grace watched the road, but after a few minutes when nothing happened and they just kept travelling along an empty road, she turned her attention to other thoughts. 'We are crossing the border now,' Paddy remarked. Again, Grace stared dutifully out of the window and, like before, they continued driving along the same empty road.

'I don't see any checkpoint!'

'There are no checkpoints,' he said, a smile crossing his face. 'Just the markings on the road. I probably didn't explain it well enough.'

'I'm sorry. It's me who didn't listen well enough,' she replied, as she looked out at the white lines on the road.

'No-o-oh, I'm rubbish at these things anyway.'

'No, you are good,' Grace insisted. 'It's me who should have been paying attention.'

'Oh no-oh, you're grand.' He stretched his hand across her seat, pointing at the white markings running along the road. 'Just keep an eye on those. When we are in the

Republic, those lines turn yellow, and all the road signs have two languages—English and Irish.'

When he started pointing out landmarks to her, Grace took it they had passed the border. He told her stories to accompany each town of interest—for a mountainous town, he told her about a tourist couple who were so taken by the landscape that they decided to move to the town; for another town, he pointed out an area where a famous poet had lived and died; and when they crossed by a sea town, he told her about a ferry that can take people around the town and how lovely it is to do when the weather was nice. 'The only problem is that we are cursed with our weather,' he concluded.

Grace continued staring out the window long after he had stopped talking, overwhelmed by the beautiful landscape they were passing, replaying the stories he had told her.

They had been travelling for a while when he glanced at her and said quietly, 'We should be in Dublin in an hour.'

Grace made a sad face. 'I have really enjoyed this journey.'

'Are you pregnant?' he asked, glancing quickly at her.

'Ex-cuse *me*?!' Grace shrieked, eyes widening.

'I just asked if you were pregnant,' he repeated, his eyes staring at the road.

'No, I'm not pregnant!' Grace retorted indignantly, waiting for him to tell her why he had asked her this question, though a squeamish part of her was afraid of the answer she might get.

'I mean, you're a good-looking girl ...' he said, smiling across at her.

'Thank you,' Grace said, still frowning at him.

'I'd like a nice-looking woman myself,' he continued, after a moment.

'I'm married,' Grace said firmly, placing her hands on her thighs. 'Well, soon to be.'

'Oh.' She thought she felt him glance at her bare fingers.

'My fiancé is Udeme. Jessica's brother ...' Grace explained.

'Oh,' he said, sounding surprised. 'I didn't know.' Without looking up, she felt him studying her, a keenness to his gaze.

'It's ok,' Grace answered awkwardly, shrugging away his apology.

'Well, if you have a friend,' he took out another business card from the compartment and held it out to Grace.

Grace took the card from him and looked at his name emblazoned in black ink—Patrick Paddy McGuinley—without taking in any other detail on the card. She tucked it into her denim pocket. Outside, it had started to rain, everywhere had turned dark. Grace looked at the rain-streaked window, her eyes switching from the red tail-lights of the cars in front to the yellow headlights of oncoming cars travelling in the opposite direction.

'We are now in Dublin,' he said. Grace moved her head dutifully in a semblance of a nod.

'Are you excited?' he asked, smiling perfunctorily—a smile so different from the smiles she had seen on his face throughout the journey, such was its lack of warmth.

Grace shrugged. There was no right way for her to answer his question. She couldn't admit she wasn't excited, and she couldn't lie and say she was either. She leaned back into her seat and listened to the sounds coming from the windscreen wipers as they fought against the lashing rain.

The next time he spoke was when he brought the car to a stop in front of a row of houses. 'Here we are!' he announced.

Grace turned to regard the view from her window. The street they were in was softly lit from lights seeping out of houses. The same lights caused the ground to glisten in the rain. Udeme's address, that she had learned, said the area was called Swords. Udeme had used the word 'estate' many times when he talked about the place. The only similarity it bore for Grace to some of the estates in Lagos was that some of the houses looked alike, but this estate had no main entry gate, and its road was devoid of potholes.

'It looks like a nice neighbourhood,' Grace said, turning from the window to consider Paddy. She saw that he had his phone in his hand.

'Yeah, it's alri,' he said unenthusiastically, scrolling through his phone. Stopping at a number and pressing the dial button, he placed the phone to his ear. 'Are you ready to go meet your fiancé?' he asked, lifting his eyebrows at her.

Grace wondered at the sudden change in his mood as she gave him a faint smile. 'I think so,' she said.

A voice came through the phone in his hand, and he said, 'We are here.' He got out of the car and by the time she could gather herself, he already had her suitcase out of the boot and was carrying it to the front door of a house. He pressed the doorbell and, without waiting for an answer, he strode back to the car.

Grace stood outside in the drizzle waiting for him. She handed Paddy his fare, the amount Udeme had told her to give him. 'Thank you very much,' she said.

'No worries,' he replied tautly.

The abruptness in his voice pleased her strangely. Was he missing her company already? Was he jealous she was going to meet another man? That would mean he was attracted to her.

Grace looked behind her at the door to distract herself from her wayward thoughts. No one had come to answer it yet.

'Ahh, someone will come to get it soon,' he said, reading her mind. He opened the car door and climbed back in. Closing the door, he wound down his side window and put his head out.

'Remember what I said, if you have any nice friend …'

Grace narrowed her eyes at him. He raised his hand in salute—was it in platitude or in farewell? Grace was not sure. She heard her name being called and turned to the voice. Behind her, she heard Paddy start his car and drive away slowly. It came to her then that it was neither platitude nor farewell that had caused his hand to be raised. Rather, Paddy was pointing her attention to Udeme, who was standing at the door.

Catastrophe

Kevin Power

It was a shock to see him in life, the great man. John Wycherly, the novelist, one of Mark's heroes—no, no, that was putting it too mildly. *Hero* didn't cover it. Wycherly's work had been a shaping force in Mark's life. At one point he had read the novels, particularly *The Apparitions* and *Faust's Love*, over and over again, as if in search of instructions—hidden messages—about how to live. More recently, he had worked various allusions to Wycherly's fiction into his own first novel, in the hope that the man himself might notice and approve.

Now here Wycherly was, stumping up the stairs to the first floor of the Central Hotel on Exchequer Street, supported by a walking stick or cane, looking as if the short climb to the landing had already exhausted him. An unassuming figure, as a lesser novelist might put it, shapeless in scarves and a vast stained coat, bewilderingly unrecognizable when compared with the suave jacket photographs of three decades ago.

'My interlocutor,' Wycherly said in a loud voice, pointing the walking stick at Mark and not smiling.

This brief performance seemed to exhaust him all over again.

Mark had been rehearsing his opening line, which was, he felt, classically simple (and which also had the virtue of being true): *It's an absolute honour to meet you.* But just as he began to speak, Wycherly abruptly huffed past him and headed for the door of the Library Bar, and the only version of his greeting Mark was able to articulate was 'Absolutely—' and as he spoke his voice sounded reedy and insufficient to his own ears. *Oh, well done, Mark,* said a familiar sneering inner voice. *Off to a fucking idiotic start, of course, of course, of course.* He ground his teeth, as he sometimes did when Clara talked about money.

But then Wycherly's mood appeared to change. 'Don't mind the bullshit,' he said, as they paused in the doorway—the doorway, which Wycherly seemed to have encountered as a sort of obstruction, barring his progress. He waved once again with the stick, which was tipped with a band of brass, like a snooker cue.

'The bullshit?' Mark said.

'The theatrical greeting,' Wycherly said. 'It's meant to put you at a disadvantage. That's why theatrical people are the way they are. They want the upper hand.'

'You don't like theatricality,' Mark said. He was reminded of what it was like to meet a famous person: how at every second you thought not about them but about yourself, about how you sounded, about what you said, about how stupid your remarks would or wouldn't seem when exposed to the special attention it was mysteriously in the power of a famous person to bestow. This remark, neutrally phrased, seemed to pass muster—though of course everything Mark said would need to be scrutinized later, in agonized retrospect, to make sure he had not embarrassed himself.

'Mm,' Wycherly said.

'And yet you've written about it so much,' Mark said.

'Starting the autopsy already, are we,' Wyckerly said. 'At least buy me a glass of wine before you make the first incision.'

It was late morning. The Library Bar was quiet. A few solitary newspaper readers occupied a few of the ancient wingback chairs. Autumn sunlight, a glimmering dove-grey, fell weakly through the leaded windows. Under his arm Mark clutched an Advance Reading Copy of *The Fatalist*, Wycherly's new one. This the newspaper had couriered to his tiny house in Ringsend a week ago, along with a sheaf of publicity materials recapitulating Wycherly's career: the prizes, translations, honorary degrees, the bestsellers, the movie adaptations … Mark also clutched his Moleskin notebook, which was supposed to contain his prepared questions, but which actually contained nothing at all.

Wycherly settled himself at a table, fussing with his scarves—he seemed to be wearing two or three of them, each of which needed to be complicatedly disentwined from one another and then in some finicky further way extricated from the capacious recesses of his enormous coat—while Mark hovered at the bar.

Covertly Mark studied the impressive face. The long jowls, the sharp nose, the calm blue eyes expressive somehow of vast interior struggles triumphantly overcome. It was, absolutely inarguably, the face of an artist. No one— no casual passer-by—could ever have mistaken Wycherly for anything else. *There sits an artist!* Mark wondered if, in thirty years, his own face would be unmistakably an artist's face. But: *Of course it fucking won't,* said the inner voice. *You only get a face like that if you spend a lifetime making art. And you haven't written anything in three years. No, wait, I'm sorry: not three years. Four. And counting.*

Mark brought two glasses of pinot noir to the table. Wycherly, divested of his scarves and coat, looked at last approximately like himself, or at least more like his jacket photographs: in his dark suit and tie, *soigné* and self-contained. He looked around and said, 'Will this be quiet enough, do you think?'

'For what?' Mark said.

The ghost of a laugh. 'I presume you have your Dictaphone, or what have you. I hope you have. I wouldn't want to trust my pearls of wisdom to the frailty of human memory.'

'I'm not really a journalist,' Mark said.

'Ah,' Wycherly said. 'That's what they all say. But what is a journalist?'

'Mm,' Mark said. He tried to think of something clever to say, and was met with only the bright glare of an empty mind. After a moment he said, 'What indeed.'

Wycherly's face became impassive. He seemed to conclude with a small sigh that he would have to do most of the conversational heavy lifting himself. 'I was a journalist for ten years,' he said. 'And I always felt like an impostor. But that's what a journalist is. An impostor. Trying to find out what these strange creatures, human beings, are up to. Like an alien sent down from Mars, with a notebook and a recording device. Asking questions. They're not really human, journalists.'

The great man had gone into professional mode—Mark recognized an old Wycherly riff. No great loss if Mark failed to record this. He could cut-and-paste it verbatim from any number of other interviews if necessary. Besides, he had now, after several panicked seconds, successfully activated the voice recording app on his phone. He set the black oblong down mistrustfully on the table between them. He saw as he did so that his hands were trembling. His head ached, his mouth was dry. Nerves, merely? *Never meet your heroes,* Clara had said, when he told her he had been asked to 'do Wycherly'. *Why,* Mark said, *because they always disappoint you?* Clara said: *No, because they make you disappointed in yourself.*

Which was supposed to mean what? Mark had shaken his head, knowing that he could not possibly refuse the assignment. Wycherly! The finest living prose stylist in English! And the money: €600 for two thousand words. He needed the money, urgently. And Clara had agreed, of course, that this was so.

And Mark had not slept: this was another problem. An ongoing problem. He lay down in bed at night beside Clara and closed his eyes and at once a circus carousel of terrors and recriminations wheezed and jangled luridly to life in his head. *No money no second novel no job no future,* said the circus horses, in a whinnying monotone, *no money no second novel no job no future. Everything you write is garbage.* Who could sleep through that? In the mornings he felt like a flat battery in some futile machine. Clara worked in an office and fell asleep every night, effortlessly, in five minutes. Mark lay beside her, comparing his stalled career with the careers of other writers. Wycherly was his habitual comparator. First novel at twenty-seven. Second novel at twenty-nine. And a novel every two or three years thereafter. How had he done it?

And the novels were so good—the prose so burnished, the plots so intricately built. Once, in a spirit of self-mortification, Mark had placed the paperback edition of his own novel on his desk beside a copy of *The Apparitions*. He read from each in turn, sickened by the difference in quality. Next to Wycherly, he was a lucky amateur: nothing more.

A few months ago—his insomnia briefly in abeyance— Mark had had a dream about him: about Wycherly. Nothing so unusual about that, of course. He often dreamed about writers, or writing. In the dream Mark was hammering on the door of Wycherly's house, asking to be let in. *I need help*, Mark had said. That was all he remembered.

The house he shared with Clara was a minuscule two-up-two-down, formerly a labourer's cottage. The windows were single-glazed and the bedroom was always cold. 'You were crying in your sleep,' Clara said, when he awoke from his Wycherly dream. 'Was I?' Mark said, shivering. Increasingly, Clara went for drinks after work with her friends, and came home late. Mark, alone in the house, tried to write. When of course he did not succeed, he watched TV instead.

He did not function as a writer. Occasionally he functioned as a book reviewer for the arts pages of a Sunday supplement. That was how the interview had come about. Mark was known to be a Wycherly fan.

Wycherly was looking out of the window, at the Exchequer Street crowds. Above the shop fronts the buildings were red-brick and topped with vaguely Gothic spires and crannies.

'What I mean is,' Mark said, 'I'm really just playing at being a journalist. You're the first person I've ever interviewed.'

Another faint smile. 'I'll be gentle, then.'

'Don't feel obliged,' Mark said. He sounded gruff, even hostile. When what he had meant was to be wry. This now happened frequently. He kept misjudging tone, when he spoke.

Wycherly looked at him quizzically. 'And what do you do when you're not pretending to be a journalist?'

'I write,' Mark said, after a moment. 'I've published a novel.'

'Ah,' Wycherly said. He wagged the jowly chin. 'Another member of the brotherhood. The doomed brotherhood of scriveners.'

So: Wycherly had not read his book. But of course he hadn't. Why would he? Why would he have wasted the time? Besides, it didn't matter. The man was sitting across the table. They were together, for an hour at least. Mark felt a strange sense of urgency. *Get on with it!*

'Why are we doomed?' he said.

'Oh, you know, the usual. Doomed to failure. Doomed to obscurity. It isn't really a life, putting words together in a little room. All of that.'

'But what other life has value?' Mark said.

Wycherly gave a look of long-philtrumed disapproval. 'Any other life. The man sweeping the street. Invaluable. The gentleman there behind the bar. They live in the real world. They don't waste their time speculating about shadows.'

'But they don't make anything,' Mark said. 'They don't make anything beautiful.'

Wycherly sipped his wine. 'This is a quirk of the artist's nature. The need to make something beautiful. We compete with nature. It's foolishness. The world is already beautiful. Why can't we leave it alone?'

'You didn't leave it alone,' Mark said.

A pause. Then Wycherly said, 'Look out there. The trees. The leaves. I know that trees lose their leaves for what you might call scientific-materialist reasons, evolutionary reasons. But actually I think, I assume, that the trees lose their leaves so that October will be the most beautiful time of year. The world really exists for me, at the most basic level, as an aesthetic phenomenon. I hate ugliness and I love beauty. But that doesn't make me special. In fact it makes me useless. Spending years of my life fashioning these pale imitations of reality.'

'All art is quite useless,' Mark quoted.

'Wilde knew what art was for,' Wycherly said. 'He wrote plays to make money.'

'I wanted to ask you—' Mark said.

But someone had loomed suddenly over their table. It was a middle-aged woman, in small half-moon glasses. 'Oh, I thought it was you,' she said to Wycherly in a confidential tone. 'I loved the last one. Absolutely loved it.'

'Thank you very much,' Wycherly said.

The woman glanced at Mark. Not recognizing him, she smiled vaguely. Then moved on, into one of the book-lined snugs or antechambers. Wycherly's expression was neutral. Mark watched the woman, still visible through a doorway, as she settled herself on a couch. In one of those little side-rooms, five years ago, Mark had met his publisher for the first time. The atmosphere of the Library Bar had seemed to him then like the atmosphere of civilisation itself. To sit in the big soft chairs, meeting your publisher! While all the ordinary people, the non-artists, the civilians, passed by on the street outside, mired in the unwritten, in the unpublished world—condemned to mundanity! Mark had ordered Laphroaig, neat. A peaty Scotch: it seemed to him a writerly drink. And now that he was going to be a writer, he thought that he had better gather his writerly accessories, his defences. He would need to be prepared for his new life.

Mark coughed. 'I wanted to ask you,' he said, 'about your second novel—about the period between *Bluebeard's Chamber* and *Misery Hill*—'

'Ah, yes,' Wycherly said. 'The early, funny ones.'

'That period,' Mark said. 'The second novel ...'

'Oh, I'd written most of *Misery Hill* by the time *Bluebeard* came out,' Wycherly said. 'I think the first one takes so long that you have a lot of stored-up energy, so you write the second one all in a rush. But that's a long time ago now. It seems very distant. Why do you ask?'

'I seem to remember,' Mark said. 'Reading somewhere, or hearing somewhere, that you'd gone through a crisis.'

Wycherly chuckled. 'Oh yes, a crisis. Many crises. Life is a crisis. What do they say? The full catastrophe. Wife, kids, death, the works. We write because we're in crisis, and because we're always in crisis, we always write.'

'But I'm trying to get at a specific crisis, in your work, in your life—'

Wycherly now looked at him with unwonted keenness. But said nothing.

'You couldn't write,' Mark prompted. 'Or you couldn't get a book going properly, or ...'

Wycherly nodded slowly. 'After *Mirabelle*,' he said. 'Oh yes. I found ... I found I'd reached, I suppose, a point of rest. After five books, I had ... I had said much of what was in me, or so I thought. I tended my garden for six months. It was very satisfying. You could get real results. Pruning the rosebushes, and so on. Then one day I looked up and I was back at my desk. Back in the land of shadows.'

'And that was *The Apparitions*,' Mark said.

'Mm,' Wycherly said.

'How,' Mark said, and coughed. 'How did you feel, during that time? Were you afraid it was, I don't know. Gone forever?'

Wycherly held his wine glass in both hands. Again, he looked through the window, at the spired red-brick roofs. 'When Joyce was in his twenties,' he said, 'he went to see Yeats in London. You know, letter of introduction in his pocket. They chatted about books, money. Art. Disagreed, of course. Joyce said, "You are too old for me to help you".'

Mark waited.

'I seem to remember that Yeats was around thirty-seven, at the time,' Wycherly said.

'Do you mean,' Mark said, 'it was a question of getting older? That the problems sort of solved themselves?'

He seemed to be leaning across the table. His arms were folded tightly at his chest.

Wycherly set his wine glass down carefully on its circular beermat. 'Joyce had his pride,' he said. 'That's very important for an artist. Pride. Joyce was saying, I don't need your help. I can do it on my own.'

'Yes but there must come a point,' Mark said, 'when you *can't* ... When there's a sort of guild system, you know, you offer help and advice to the younger artist ... When they're in need.'

Wycherly pressed his lips together. After a moment, he nodded at the book on the table: *The Fatalist*, by John Wycherly.

'You haven't asked me anything about that yet,' he said.

'No,' Mark said.

Indeed, he had not. And for a very good reason: he had not read it. He had not been able to bring himself to read it. He could not get past the perfect first lines: *Venice. I do not know why I have come here. Perhaps to escape my guilt at last, though of course that diligent ghost is always with me, and he will find me here, or I will find him, yes, we will meet by chance in some arcaded street, the long-familiar figure, attired now in Harlequin's motley, or in the long black cloak and beaked white mask of the plague doctor ...* For five days Mark had carried the book from room to room, unopened. Last night he had lain awake—he had seemed somehow even more awake than usual—thinking about these lines, about the smooth facility with which Wycherly seemed able to generate such paragraphs, and about his own aborted manuscripts, his dull trudging sentences, his empty aperçus. Venice. Of course Wycherly knew Venice. Had lived there, probably, when he was younger: the cosmopolitan intellectual on tour. Mark had never visited Venice, had never lived outside Ireland. And why not? Because he was a coward, and an idiot about money, and because he was too stupid ever to have thought of just *going to Venice* ... A great grey tide of panic seeped outward from these reflections. It seemed, this tide, to spoil, item by item, the physical world itself: the blue-grey bedroom, the pale orange-lit street beyond, all spoiled, polluted. *No no no.* The tide must be resisted. Mark issued himself with a stern order: *Just get up and make a cup of coffee and read the damn book.* But in the kitchen, with the lights on, everything seemed more spoiled still. It was 3 a.m. The house ticked around him, settling. He opened the cutlery drawer and took out a paring knife with a short, curved blade. He pressed the flat side of the blade against his left wrist, where the artery pulsed close to the surface. But this notion, too, was spoiled, there was nothing meaningful about it, as there was nothing meaningful about anything. The knife was pathetic, like everything else. It was pathetic to be a man in a kitchen at 3 a.m., holding a knife to your wrist, as if proceeding to the next logical step in this sequence could change anything or matter in any way. He put the knife back in the drawer and went back to bed and lay still, feeling his eyes dry out as he stared unblinking into the darkness.

Wycherly was waiting for him to speak. Mark forced himself to relax—to sit back in his chair. The effort exhausted him. Around them the Library Bar was filling up with lunchtime customers.

'I'm stuck,' Mark said. 'I'm badly stuck. I don't know what I'm doing, how to … How to live, I suppose. Not just how to write, but they're, they're, they're the same thing, aren't they, they're connected? I needed … I can't seem to *see* clearly, I can't seem to … I don't know, I mean, you always say … What I wanted to … To ask you …' Mark hiccupped, surprising himself. What was he saying?

Wycherly looked away, and the corners of his mouth turned down, as if he had seen something embarrassing, or distasteful.

Mark tried to laugh. 'I need, I wanted your advice. Your books …'

'It's been very pleasant,' Wycherly said. He was gathering his scarves. He indicated Mark's copy of *The Fatalist*. 'Do you want me to sign it? It's Mark, isn't it?' Mark passed him the book. From a pocket of his shapeless coat Wycherly produced a pen that gleamed expensively, and bent with concentration over the title page. For what seemed a long time he wrote—looping words. Then closed the book and left it on the table. As he wrapped himself in his manifold layers, and groped for the handle of his walking stick, the sunlight through the windows briefly brightened, and Mark apprehended for the first time in the changed light Wycherly's tired grey face and grey hair, the hopelessly rumpled coat, the stilted movements—favouring the left leg or hip, grimacing in pain, shuffling awkwardly. There was the truth. Wycherly was an old man. *You are too old for me to help you.* They shook hands. Wycherly departed.

The voice app on Mark's phone was still recording. He had managed to preserve in digital form less than ten minutes of material for his interview. He pressed STOP and was given two options: SAVE. DELETE. He pressed DELETE. He picked up *The Fatalist* and turned to the title page. *To Mark*, the inscription read, *with best wishes, John W.* He would need to piece the interview together using excerpts from other interviews and his own reflections on the books. It would be a botch job. But so what? So was everything. He needed the money. He picked up his empty notebook and his copy of *The Fatalist*. He would go home, write the piece, file it on time, and after it appeared in print he would never read another word of Wycherly's ever again.

Tramlines

Caitriona Lally

Afternoons were the worst since she'd had the baby; mornings you could fill with tasks, however pointless, but the afternoons bloated indifferently. She'd never been a coffee drinker but had taken up caffeine since producing a baby who didn't nap for more than thirty minutes at a time. Days and nights were oozing into each other; some days she thought if she didn't give herself a project, she might never put her socks on. Today's project was to walk the green Luas tramline from the northside terminus at Broombridge into town. This line had only crossed the city a few years ago and it was still a novelty to see her postcode sliced into stops and zones. She pointed the buggy west for Broombridge, deviating slightly to buy a bun from the local bakery. She took her change from a gruff woman in a hairnet; no matter how pleasant she was, this woman never grunted more than the briefest of exchanges—she thought once she had the baby, she'd have extra traction with the woman, but the dourness levels remained the same.

When the Luas had first crossed the city, she had cringed at the people from the other side of the river day-tripping the new line. They couldn't hide their astonishment that there was a world beyond Ranelagh or Dundrum, that 'some parts of the northside are *actually ok*', that there could be redbrick houses outside of the south suburbs. They made her feel like a zoo specimen on a field trip with the captors: here be the natives, and she'd gotten the urge to hiss and snap at them.

Broombridge to Dominick: the first five stops were off-road, so if she wanted to follow the track, she could only walk down the closest street. It seemed important to follow the line from the beginning, for achievement's sake. She headed down Bannow Road, it was the nearest she could get to the first stage of the tramline, running parallel. When the road curved, there was nothing she could do but head wide for Fassaugh Road and meet the Luas at the Cabra stop. There were empty sleeves of sleeping pills planted among weeds and stones at the verge of the footpath, Zimmos the people who dealt in them called them.

In the adjoining park she passed silver bullets scattered around the remains of a fire; the teenagers were at the laughing gas again. When she'd first moved here it was all blackened spoons and syringes, maybe you could trace a city's drug evolution through its discarded accoutrements. She'd had practice arranging her face in a neutral expression as she passed drug deals—the pram surely gave her unthreatening credentials—but she wondered yet again if this was the right place to bring up children; what had seemed the right side of edgy in her pre-baby days now seemed downright foolhardy.

She had to take a block parallel to follow the Luas to the Phibsborough stop. Phibsborough/Phibsboro was a disputed answer to the quiz question about the five suburbs of Dublin that end in the letter o, but they had to leave out the *ugh* at the end to manoeuvre their way to that answer. (Pimlico was the one people mostly left out; everyone got Marino, Portobello, Rialto.) She hadn't gone to a pub quiz in ages, she dreaded having to go to a team-bonding quiz for work when her maternity leave finished. Her brain had fogged and dulled since having the baby, the words were in there but it took so long to retrieve them that she often stopped speaking mid-sentence and assumed the person she was talking to would know what she meant.

She crossed the North Circular Road to take Rathdown, a block from the tramline but it'd have to do. She had looked up the North Circular South Circular roads on a map once; they had made two vague circling waves around the city but hadn't quite met full circle, unlike the London versions which joined impressively in a fine circle with tiny peaks through it. London seemed to do everything Dublin couldn't.

At Grangegorman, she headed for the grounds of the old psychiatric hospital that was being turned into an institute of education. She had a joke ready, about replacing one kind of institutionalization with another, but it had been renamed a technological university before she'd got a chance to make the joke, and maybe the joke was the wrong side of right. A banjaxed car clamp rested against the entrance. The first time she'd seen one of these battered yellow triangles she couldn't think what it was, it was like seeing a distant acquaintance in an unfamiliar context. It was only months later when she saw a man huffing and grunting as he yanked the clamp off the tyre that she realized what it was she'd seen.

Inside the campus, benches were laid out at intervals, wooden benches that were too deep to be comfortable but maybe that was the point. She couldn't sit because the baby would scream so she did her usual lap of the grounds. She passed the patients smoking outside the hospital, the same few who were there every time she passed and she waved to them. She always mentioned what the weather was doing and then berated herself for not finding anything more original to say. She looped around the sports pitches, watching the baby closely for signs of heavy eyes. He was fighting sleep as he always did, so she started shushing as she walked. Sometimes she shushed so much her lips ached. Sometimes she shushed when the baby wasn't around because it was all she knew to say. As she passed the playground—unable to even imagine the baby being big enough to use the swing—the screeches of children seemed to lull him to sleep better than her shushing did, yet another facet of her parenting that would be more successfully outsourced. She raced up the gravelly path—no time for the tarmacked buggy slope now—to the benches and sat panting, the baby thoroughly asleep after his bumpy ride. She pulled out her book. A half-hour was all she got, you could set your clock by this child, her mother said, and you surely could. It was her only reading time so she read, militantly.

The baby woke bang on thirty minutes later as he always did, with a bellow. This was hell-time, the part of the day when no amount of singing or cuddling or shushing or cooing would soothe him. She made comical faces at him as she pushed the buggy but he was wholly unimpressed so she picked up the pace and began to jog. This eased the roaring a little; it wasn't so much mollified he looked as marginally less outraged. But, she realized, the only way to halt the roars was to get up a mad caper down the road, a fierce trot, the bumpier the road the better. The pram was a cheap model, a light, flimsy yoke with cruel suspension that lifted off the slightest bump and thwacked back down on the path, the harder the thwack the better it seemed, it was the only thing that made the child chuckle. She set off at a desperate trot around the campus and he was amused for a while but no, he wanted bigger thrills, rougher surfaces so out the gate she ran. She lashed across the road and onto the new path that hugged the Luas tracks, buffered by the old hospital. No, this path was too new, too smooth, so she zigzagged the buggy, buffeting it up and down, and the baby's bored squawks shrilled into happy shrieks. She turned onto the road that cut Broadstone bus garage in two, keeping a side-eye out for lurching double deckers swerving in and out of service, before launching the pram down the hill. She took a sharp left and slowed to a halt to let the Luas cross, the one she'd heard trundle down the slope to the stop, but the baby started squawking again. As soon as the arse of the tram had passed, she sheered on, swerving into the quieter uphill part of Phibsborough Road, beside those grand old houses that made her think of drawing rooms and brandy and cigars. She swung the pram at the potholes and bumps and the baby laughed, she was sweating now but anything less than full pelt enraged him so she heaved onwards. *Mind yourself and your new body,* the parenting books had advised after having a baby, they hadn't this kind of a caper in mind. She rejoined the main road at the late bar where she'd gone to the occasional twenty-first or later a thirtieth, the kind of place where anything could happen. It seemed a lifetime ago now. She tried to imagine the baby as a drunk student but couldn't get beyond the teething years.

By the time she passed the fire station, the child had got up an awful racket which tore at her eardrums. He didn't seem to like the slight of the uphill, maybe he wanted more of a gradient. Back around she swerved, bouncing the pram and sprinting back the way she'd come, looking behind as she ran for a break in traffic before pegging it across the road. Maybe this side would be more to his taste. The path here was narrower and required more concentration to avoid oncoming pedestrians but on she ran, past the student accommodation before skewing suddenly around the corner onto Western Way. The baby seemed to object to the new direction, maybe it was too far from the tram, and screeched until she lunged across the road and down Dominick Street, back to the tramlines. She passed the pub on the corner, the one she went to often enough she could be said to frequent it. You could sit in the corner of the L-window and watch Luases in both directions and forget you had to be anywhere. It was an ordinary friendly pub, the kind you'd drink pints in and know not to ask for cocktails. Loaves of bread had been delivered and left outside, more white than brown, the right kind of ratio.

By now there was another tram passing and the baby let out a happy gurgle. Down Dominick Street she ran, keeping level with the Luas, pumping sweat now, feeling her legs back to her marathon days, when she had a body that did what she wanted it to do. The passengers in the tram looked out, a man waved—at her or the baby she wasn't sure—others looked bemused. She ran the length of the street but the child got up a ferocious wail. The pitch of the cry sheared her innards, *Christ, anything to make it stop.* She swerved the buggy around the corner onto Parnell Street, past the former pop-up park that was now a building site. Buildings seemed to pop up these days (or maybe that was another sign of age, like doctors and guards seeming too young to be in positions of authority). When she had gone to town the first time after the baby was born there were blocks and blocks of new student accommodation and new boutique hotels being built. Doughnuts had replaced cupcakes, Oirish souvenir tat-shops had multiplied, and she was shocked at how quickly a city could become unfamiliar.

A car beeped but she didn't turn to look, just shushed the baby before he started up his screech, before flinging the buggy wildly down the tracks. This was no good, a direct track-line was deemed unsatisfactory now, the bar had been set unfeasibly high, so she weaved the buggy over and back across each track. It wasn't so much the bump as the dip on each side that he liked, chuckling as the buggy dropped and rose again. She was going as fast as she could, the baby's giggles were coming gapless, she pushed her legs until they felt like somebody else's, like they didn't belong to her, like her running youth had returned to her. She could hear, or more, feel the Luas behind her now, the driver giving a few gentle taps on the horn but hell, if she could birth this lad she could out-run a Luas. She ripped across O'Connell Street where the tracks parted and merged, heading straight for Parnell St East. She knew the driver had to stop, knew she could win and win she did, even if it was a race of her own devising with a result only she could control. As she passed the stop, she saw concerned faces and let her legs slow, like the moment of crossing the finish line on the track when she was a teenager, a conscious move to stop something that had been unconscious just a moment ago. Her legs began to wobble, her breathing came in juddering blurts, she pulled in beside the bookies and bent double to snatch a breath, grasping the buggy handle to steady herself. A man smoking outside the bookies hunkered down into her vision.

'Are you all right, luv?'

'Fine, she gasped, never better.'

She gave him a thumbs up and uprighted herself. The baby stared at her face, no doubt puce and sweaty, and scrunched up his own before settling into an almighty shriek. This was one of the aspects of parenting that the more experienced parents who constantly entreated her to *enjoy every minute* had clearly forgotten in their blurry nostalgia.

She decided that the Parnell stop was town official, that she'd completed her project so she could head for home. Lathered in sweat turning cold, she trudged up Parnell Square pointing the pram for Phibsboro. She got that familiar tight feeling of dread, the realization that what used to come easily now was almost impossible. She wanted to go to a café; she wasn't looking for a night on the lash ending in Abrakebabra, all she wanted was to drink a cup of coffee in a café. A gaunt man stepped out of a doorway on Berkeley Street.

'Have you two euro for a hostel, please?'

The *please* sounded so desperate that she rooted in her wallet but could only find a fiver. She handed it to him and started to ask for change but he'd gone, limping a hop and skip, making more speed than he looked capable of.

She passed the two new cafés on the North Circular Road, which seemed to be vying for the most exposed brickwork, the lowest case signage font, the smashiest avocado. These places were usually unwelcoming to buggies and their pushers but as she passed the first one, she peered in the window. The man behind the counter smiled. Maybe she wouldn't be a pariah if the baby cried—that's how low her bar was. Sometimes the absence of hostility counted as kindness. She pushed the buggy in the door backwards, winced at the pounding music, and made to walk out again until she looked at the baby and saw his eyes widen, his whole face unfurling into a smile. He tossed his little head to the beat with such vigour that she decided all the parenting books and expert opinions were worthless; the child was bored witless of prescribed nursery rhymes and baby-sized melodies. Her mind heaved with all the other received wisdoms and advice she'd assumed she had to obey. She ordered a coffee.

'For here or take away?'

'Here, please.'

And she pushed the buggy to the table nearest the door, in case of a necessary sudden exit. Baby steps, she told herself.

Notes on the Authors

Brendan Behan was born in Dublin in 1923 into an Irish Republican family. He was arrested at the age of sixteen for complicity in an act of terrorism and was sentenced to three years borstal in England. He subsequently received a fourteen-year prison sentence in Ireland for republican activities, serving almost five years before being released as part of a general amnesty in 1947. Behan began writing when in prison and had poems and stories published in various magazines, in Irish and in English. His plays include *The Quare Fellow* (1954), the Irish-language play *An Giall* (1958), and the adapted translation *The Hostage* (also 1958). Behan's other publications include the celebrated autobiographical novel *Borstal Boy* (1958), the sketchbook *Brendan Behan's Island* (1962), and *Confessions of an Irish Rebel* (1964). He struggled with alcoholism, and his final years were marked by poor health. A collection of his short stories, *After the Wake*, was published posthumously in 1981. He died in 1964.

Elizabeth Bowen was born in Dublin in 1899, and was the only child of an Anglo-Irish family that settled in Cork in the seventeenth century. She was one of the most acclaimed writers of the mid-twentieth century, and her novels include *The*

Last September (1929), *The House in Paris* (1935), *The Death of the Heart* (1938), *The Heat of the Day* (1949), *A World of Love* (1955), and *Eva Trout* (1969). Bowen was also the author of several volumes of short stories, including *Ann Lee's* (1926), *The Cat Jumps* (1933), *Look at All Those Roses* (1941), *The Demon Lover* (1945), and *A Day in the Dark* (1965). Her nonfiction prose includes the family chronicle *Bowen's Court* (1942), a childhood memoir *Seven Winters* (1943), and a history of Dublin's Shelbourne Hotel (1951). Bowen worked as an air-raid warden during the Second World War, and she produced some of the most famous literary depictions of London during the Blitz. She was awarded a CBE for services to literature in 1948, and she was made a Companion of Literature by the Royal Society of Literature in 1965. She died in 1973.

George Egerton is the pseudonym of Mary Chavelita Dunne Bright. She was born in Australia in 1859 but spent much of her formative early years in Ireland. Egerton was a short story writer, a novelist, and a playwright; she was also a translator of note, producing the first English-language translation of Knut Hamsun's novel *Hunger* in 1899. Her short fiction includes the enormously successful, and deeply controversial, volumes *Keynotes* (1893) and *Discords* (1895), as well as *Symphonies* (1897) and *Flies in Amber* (1905). Forthright and politically engaged, Egerton was a key figure in the late nineteenth and early twentieth century New Woman movement, and her work frequently explores such issues as sexual freedom, financial independence, and the importance of female education. She travelled widely but lived in England for most of her adult life. She died in 1945.

Mirsad Ibišević was born in the former Yugoslavia Republic of Bosnia and Herzegovina, and lived in Sarajevo, where he was badly injured in the war in 1993. In 1994 the Irish government allowed him entry to Ireland for medical treatment and he was subsequently offered a permanent visa to stay in the country. He has worked as a qualified fitness instructor, a taxi driver, and an actor, appearing in several films and television series. His novel, *TUNEL*, was published in 2022.

James Joyce was born in Dublin in 1882. His works include the innovative short-story collection *Dubliners* (1914), the semi-autobiographical novel *A Portrait of the Artist as a Young Man* (1916), the modernist masterpiece *Ulysses* (1922), and the experimental novel *Finnegans Wake* (1939). Joyce had an extremely difficult but also an artistically enduring relationship with his native city. He first left Dublin in 1902, but returned the following year because of his mother's terminal illness. There, he met the woman who would become the most important figure in his life, Nora Barnacle. Their first date (on 16 June 1904) was later commemorated by Joyce as the day on which *Ulysses* is set; that date is now remembered as Bloomsday, named for the protagonist of Joyce's novel, Leopold Bloom. Joyce and Nora Barnacle left Dublin in 1904; together, they lived a peripatetic life, moving between Trieste, Rome, Paris, and Zürich. He died in 1941.

Caitriona Lally's debut novel, *Eggshells*, won the 2018 Rooney Prize for Irish Literature and a Lannan Literary Fellowship for Fiction in 2019, and her second novel, *Wunderland*, was published in 2021. She currently holds the inaugural Rooney Writer Fellowship at the Trinity Long Room Hub Arts and

Humanities Research Institute. She lives in Dublin with her young family.

John McGahern was born in Dublin in 1934 and grew up in County Leitrim. He worked as a schoolteacher before controversially losing his job after his second novel, *The Dark* (1965), was banned by the Irish Censorship Board. He was the author of six novels, including *The Barracks* (1963), *Amongst Women* (1990), and *That They May Face the Rising Sun* (2002), and his short-story collections include *Nightlines* (1971), *Getting Through* (1978), and *High Ground* (1985). McGahern's *Collected Stories* was published in 1992; this was revised and expanded as *Creatures of the Earth* in 2006. McGahern also wrote plays for radio, television, and the stage; these were published posthumously as *The Rockingham Shoot and Other Dramatic Writings* (2018). His collected reviews and essays were published under the title *Love of the World* (2009), and his *Collected Letters* appeared in 2021. McGahern was the recipient of numerous awards and prizes, including the Chevalier de l'Ordre des Arts et des Lettres. *Memoir* was published shortly before his death in 2006.

Val Mulkerns was born in Dublin 1925. She was an associate editor of the influential Irish literary journal *The Bell* in the early 1950s, and was the author of the novels *A Time Outworn* (1951) and *A Peacock Cry* (1954). Mulkerns stepped back from creative writing in the mid-1950s to raise a family; around this time she began a long-running association as a freelance journalist with the national newspaper *The Evening Press*. Her debut volume of short stories, *Antiquities*, was published in 1978, and was followed by the collections

An Idle Woman (1980) and *A Friend of Don Juan* (1988). After a thirty-year break, two more novels were produced: *The Summerhouse* (1984) and *Very Like a Whale* (1986). Mulkerns was a founding member of Aosdána, the association for Irish artists, and a selection of her short stories, *Memory and Desire*, was published the year of her death, in 2018.

Éilís Ní Dhuibhne was born in Dublin. Author of more than thirty books, her work includes *The Dancers Dancing* (1999), *Fox, Swallow, Scarecrow* (2007), and *The Shelter of Neighbours* (2012). Her most recent books are *Twelve Thousand Days: A Memoir* (shortlisted for the Michel Déon Award, 2020), *Little Red and Other Stories* (2020), and the edited essay collection *Look! It's a Woman Writer! Irish Literary Feminisms 1970–2020* (2021). She has been the recipient of many literary awards, including the Pen Award for an Outstanding Contribution to Irish Literature. In 2020 she held the prestigious Burns Scholarship at Boston College. She is a member of Aosdána and is President of the Folklore of Ireland Society.

Caitlín Nic Íomhair is an academic and writer. She regularly publishes fiction, criticism, and personal essays in Irish, and she is currently working on a composite novel. Her poems were featured in the Gallery Press anthology *Calling Cards* (2018), alongside English translations by the writer Colette Bryce.

Dara Ó Conaola comes from the Aran Islands, County Galway. He is the author of ten books, the latest being a bilingual book of poetry and songs, *Ag Caint le Synge – Talking to*

Synge (2020), which includes a CD of readings and singing. His collection of stories, *Night Ructions*, with a translation by Gabriel Rosenstock, was launched at the 1990 *Sunday Times* Festival of Literature. Stage adaptations of his work include *Misiún ar Muir – Sea Mission*, shown at the Taibhdhearc Theatre, Galway, and also at Expo 1992 in Seville, Spain. Some of his poems have been set to music and recorded by singer Lasairfhíona Ní Chonaola. He is currently working on a new bilingual collection of short stories.

Mary O'Donnell is the author of eight poetry collections, including *Unlegendary Heroes* (1998), *Those April Fevers* (2015), and *Massacre of the Birds* (2020). She has also written four novels, including *Where They Lie* (2014) and her debut *The Light Makers* (1992, reissued in 2017), and three short fiction collections: *Strong Pagans* (1991), *Storm over Belfast* (2008), and *Empire* (2018). 'My Mother in Drumlin Country', published in *New Hibernia Review*, was listed among the Notable Essays and Literary Nonfiction of 2017 in *Best American Essays* (Mariner). A member of Aosdána, she holds a PhD in Creative Writing from University College Cork. She has completed a new novel, due for publication in 2023.

Liam O'Flaherty was born on Inishmore in the Aran Islands in 1896. He was a prolific novelist and short-story writer, and he also wrote several volumes of autobiography. Amongst his best novels are *The Informer* (1925), which was subsequently adapted into an acclaimed film by John Ford in 1935, as well as *The Assassin* (1928), *Skerrett* (1932), *Famine* (1937), and *Insurrection* (1950). His short-story collections include *Spring Sowing* (1924), *The Tent* (1926), and *The*

Mountain Tavern (1929). A native Irish speaker, O'Flaherty published mainly in English; his Irish-language writings include the short story collection *Dúil* (1952, translated as *Desire*). O'Flaherty's work frequently fell foul of the Irish Censorship Board in the 1930s and 1940s, and was banned on the grounds of indecency. He returned to Ireland in the early 1950s, having travelled extensively. He died in 1984.

Melatu Uche Okorie was born in Engugu, Nigeria, and has been living in Ireland for many years. Her short stories have been published in numerous anthologies, including most recently *Being Various: New Irish Short Stories* (2019, ed. Lucy Caldwell) and *The Art of the Glimpse: 100 Irish Short Stories* (2020, ed. Sinéad Gleeson). Her debut volume of stories, *This Hostel Life*, was published in 2018, and was shortlisted for an Irish Book Award; it was subsequently adapted into an operatic work by the Irish National Opera. 'Arrival' is her newest work.

Kevin Power is the author of two novels, *Bad Day in Blackrock* (2008) and *White City* (2021), and one book of criticism, *The Written World* (2022). He has written for *The New Yorker* Page Turner blog, *The Guardian*, *The Irish Times*, *The Dublin Review*, *Los Angeles Review of Books*, *The Stinging Fly*, and many other places. He won the Rooney Prize for Irish Literature in 2009 and has twice been shortlisted for an Irish Book Award. He is Assistant Professor of Literary Practice in the School of English, Trinity College Dublin.

James Stephens was born in Dublin, probably in 1880. He is best known as the author of two books that were both published in 1912: the dark urban fairy tale *The Charwoman's*

Daughter, and the genre-defying comic novel *The Crock of Gold*. His prose fiction also includes *The Demi-Gods* (1914) and *Irish Fairy Tales* (1924), as well as the short story collections *Here Are Ladies* (1913) and *Etched in Moonlight* (1918). Stephens also wrote several volumes of poetry and was the author of a vivid first-person account of life in Dublin during the Easter Rising, *The Insurrection in Dublin* (1916). He was Registrar of the National Gallery of Ireland before moving to London in 1925. In his later life, he was a frequent contributor to BBC Radio. 'A Rhinoceros, Some Ladies, and a Horse' is the only surviving part of his autobiography, and was first published in 1946. He died in 1950.

William Trevor was born in Mitchelstown, County Cork, in 1928. He was the author of fourteen novels and three novellas, including *The Children of Dynmouth* (1976), *Fools of Fortune* (1983), *Reading Turgenev* (1991), *Felicia's Journey* (1994), *The Story of Lucy Gault* (2002), and *Love and Summer* (2009). He was also a highly distinguished short story writer, and his eleven volumes of short stories include *The Ballroom of Romance* (1972), *The News from Ireland* (1986), *After Rain* (1996), *The Hill Bachelors* (2000), and *Cheating at Canasta* (2007). A final volume of stories, *Last Stories*, was published posthumously in 2018. Trevor was the recipient of many awards and prizes and was shortlisted for the Booker Prize four times. He received the David Cohen Literature Prize in 1999, and he was awarded an honorary knighthood for services to literature in 2002. He died in 2016.

Further Reading

Guidebooks

Top 10 Dublin: DK Eyewitness Guides (Dorling Kindersley, 2020). Succinct guide to many of Dublin's attractions, which is organized clearly and efficiently. Categories listed include Top 10 Arts Venues and Top 10 Things to do for Free.

Lonely Planet Dublin, by Fionn Davenport, twelfth edition (Lonely Planet, 2020). Most recent edition of the hugely popular *Lonely Planet* guide, which includes extensive information on the cultural life of the capital city, as well as maps, recommendations, and insider advice.

Secret Dublin: An Unusual Guide, by Pól Ó Conghaile, third edition (Jonglez, 2020). Idiosyncratic travel guide that avoids the conventional tourist trail, directing visitors instead to such attractions as King George IV's footprints, the inner sanctum of a Freemason's Hall, and vintage radio in one of Dublin's Martello Towers.

History and Reference Books about Dublin

Stones of Dublin: A History of Dublin in Ten Buildings, by Lisa Marie Griffith (Collins Press, 2014). Ingenious book, which charts the history of the city through ten of its most famous sites. Buildings explored include Christ Church Cathedral, the GPO, Dublin Castle, St James's Gate, Kilmainham Gaol, and Trinity College Dublin.

Dublin: The Making of a Capital City, by David Dickson (Profile Books, 2014). Cornucopia of information, which is detailed, lucid, and compelling. Performs the rare feat of being both scholarly and accessible; and unlikely to be surpassed as the history of Dublin for years to come.

Dublin: The Story of a City, by Stephen Conlin and Peter Harbison (O'Brien Press, 2016). Beautifully produced book, telling the story of the city through a combination of artwork and text. Includes lovely recreations of buildings, streetscapes, and areas at key points in their development.

Dublin: A New Illustrated History, by John Gibney (Collins, 2018). Lavishly designed history, bringing Dublin's past to life through anecdotes about personalities, architecture, literature, and song, from prehistoric settlements to the Vikings, and from colonial rule to the digital age.

Three Castles Burning: A History of Dublin in Twelve Streets, by Donal Fallon (New Island, 2022). Lively social history, inspired by Fallon's popular podcast 'Three Castles Burning', which seeks to understand the development of Dublin through the significance of a dozen of its streets.

Dublin: A Writer's City, by Chris Morash (Cambridge University Press, 2023). Engrossing 'book-lover's map of this unique city', which pays tribute to Dublin's status as a great city of literature. Informed and lucid, with a rich collection of illustrations, images, and maps.

Anthologies and Short Story Collections about Dublin

Dubliners, by James Joyce, edited by Jeri Johnson (1914; Oxford University Press, 2000). Seminal volume of fifteen stories, which provides glimpses into the lives of ordinary Dubliners at the turn of the twentieth century, concluding with the celebrated and often-reprinted long story, 'The Dead'. Joyce famously struggled to get this modernist masterpiece published and described the collection as 'a chapter of the moral history of my country'.

A New Book of Dubliners: Short Stories of Modern Dublin, edited by Ben Forkner, with a preface by Benedict Kiely (Methuen, 1988). Extensive selection of Dublin-based stories, charting 'a thriving tradition' of writing across a seventy-year period. Includes some wonderful choices but is marred by the fact that only one woman writer (Mary Lavin) is represented; also includes a lengthy introductory essay that is dominated by Joyce.

Dublines, edited by Katie Donovan and Brendan Kennelly (Bloodaxe Books, 1996). Eclectic miscellany of poems, extracts, fragments, and tales, which is intended, in the words of its editors, to 'permit Dublin to do what it's best at: talk itself into existence'. Material is organized innovatively and with a measure of irreverence.

New Dubliners, edited by Oona Frawley (New Island, 2005). Wonderful collection of eleven stories, marking a century since Joyce embarked on the book that would become *Dubliners*. Includes work by an impressive selection of Irish short story writers, and offers fresh perspectives on the city, and its citizens, in the early twenty-first century.

If Ever You Go: A Map of Dublin in Poetry and Song, edited by Pat Boran and Gerard Smyth (Dedalus Press, 2014). Lyrical mapping of the city by a diverse collection of poets, street artists, and songwriters. The title comes from a Patrick Kavanagh poem, 'If ever you go to Dublin town'. The collection was the One Dublin One Book choice in 2014.

Dubliners 100: Fifteen New Stories Inspired by the Original, edited by Thomas Morris (Tramp Press, 2014). Stunning collection of stories by some of Ireland's finest contemporary prose writers published to coincide with the centenary of *Dubliners*. Stories are offered as 'cover versions' of Joyce's work. Consequently, although they bear the same titles as Joyce's stories, and are presented in the same order, each is highly original and does not constitute a mere re-writing of the original texts.

Novels about Dublin

Ulysses, by James Joyce, edited by Sam Slote, Marc A. Mamigonian, and John Turner, third edition (1922; Alma Classics, 2017). Iconic text by Dublin's most accomplished novelist. *Ulysses* unfolds across a summer's day in Dublin in 1904 (16 June, 'Bloomsday'), and focuses on the lives of three of the city's inhabitants, Leopold and Molly Bloom, and Stephen Dedalus. Ambitious, experimental, provocative, and utterly humane, the novel is one of the great achievements in modern art.

At Swim-Two-Birds, by Flann O'Brien (1939; Penguin, 2000). Riotous comic novel, which is exhilarating and multi-layered. One of the novel's several storylines features a lazy undergraduate struggling to write in the grim world that was lower-middle-class Dublin in the late 1930s. This narrative enables and is subsequently overrun by other storylines, which are populated by a motley cast of characters, including cowboys, demons, drunks, legendary heroes, and figures from Old Irish poetry.

Strumpet City, by James Plunkett (1969; Gill & Macmillan, 2013). Classic work of social realism, which provides a panoramic view of the city against the backdrop of industrial unrest in the early twentieth century. Focuses especially upon the plight of the destitute and the working class during the extended labour strike that has become known as the Lockout. *Strumpet City* was adapted for Irish television in 1980 by the Dublin playwright Hugh Leonard. The novel was the One Dublin One Book choice on the centenary of the 1913 Lockout in 2013.

The Country Girls Trilogy, by Edna O'Brien (1986; Faber & Faber, 2019). Enormously influential series of books, which were the subject of indecent controversy on publication. The trilogy comprises *The Country Girls* (1960), *The Lonely Girl* (1962), and *Girls in Their Married Bliss* (1964), and is elegant, honest, and brave. It follows two friends as they move from rural Ireland in the 1950s to Dublin and then to London. *The Country Girls Trilogy* was the One Dublin One Book choice in 2019.

The Barrytown Trilogy, by Roddy Doyle (1993; Vintage, 2013). Hugely popular trilogy, consisting of *The Commitments* (1987), *The Snapper* (1990), and *The Van* (1991), which is driven by energetic, often colourful dialogue, and which effectively combines humour and social critique. Each of the novels was successfully adapted to film, and *The Barrytown Trilogy* was the One Dublin One Book choice in 2015.

Hood, by Emma Donoghue (1995; HarperPerennial, 2011). Sensitive novel, exploring a Dubliner's attempts to come to terms with the sudden death of her erstwhile lover. Donoghue's lesbian romance is variously delicate, erotic, witty, and sad. It is one of several novels that broke new ground in its representation of same-sex relationships and has proved especially empowering for the LGBTQ+ community in Ireland.

Tara Road, by Maeve Binchy (Orion, 1998). Enduringly popular romance, which tells the story of two women (one from Dublin, one from the USA) who swap houses for a short period in an attempt to escape their problems. *Tara Road* was an Oprah's Book Choice in 1999 and was adapted for film in 2005.

The Gathering, by Anne Enright (Jonathan Cape, 2007). Evocative novel about the trauma and the secrets that can be buried within a family's history. Enright takes on one of the most conventional paradigms in Irish literary fiction and rewrites it for a contemporary audience; this is done with characteristic daring and intelligence. A deeply moving novel, *The Gathering* was awarded the Man Booker Prize in 2007.

Fallen, by Lia Mills (Penguin, 2014). Tender novel that depicts a year in the life of a young Dubliner struggling to understand who she is following the death of her twin brother in World War One. Most of the novel unfolds against the backdrop of the Easter Rising, and brilliantly recreates the confusion and the excitement of the period. *Fallen* was the One Dublin One Book choice on the centenary of the Rising in 2016.

Publisher's Acknowledgements

1. George Egerton (pseudonym of Mary Chavelita Dunne Bright), 'Mammy', from *Flies in Amber* (Hutchinson, 1905).
2. James Joyce, 'Two Gallants', from *Dubliners* (Grant Richards, 1914).
3. Liam O'Flaherty, 'The Sniper', from *The Tent and other stories* (Jonathan Cape, 1926). Reproduced by permission of the author's estate and Peters Fraser + Dunlop.
4. Elizabeth Bowen, 'Unwelcome Idea', from *Collected Stories* (Vintage, 1983). Reproduced with permission of Curtis Brown Ltd, London, on behalf of the Literary Executors of the Estate of Elizabeth Bowen. Copyright 1941 © Elizabeth Bowen.
5. James Stephens, 'A Rhinoceros, Some Ladies, and a Horse', from *Irish Writing* 1, ed. David Marcus (1946).
6. Brendan Behan, 'The Confirmation Suit', from *Brendan Behan's Island: An Irish Sketch-book*, with drawings by Paul Hogarth (Hutchinson, 1962). Reproduced by permission of the Behan family and the Sayle Literary Agency.
7. John McGahern, 'Sierra Leone', from *Getting Through* (Faber & Faber, 1978); republished in *Creatures of the Earth: New and Selected Stories* (Faber & Faber, 2006). Reproduced by permission of the Estate of John McGahern.

8. Val Mulkerns, 'Four Green Fields', from *Antiquities* (Andre Deutsch, 1978). Reproduced by permission of Maev Kennedy and the Mulkerns family.

9. Dara Ó Conaola, 'I nGleic'. Originally published in *Comhar* 38.2 (Feabhra 1979). Translated as 'In a Pickle' by the author (2022). Reproduced by permission of the author and *Comhar*.

10. William Trevor, 'Two More Gallants', from *The News from Ireland and Other Stories* (Bodley Head, 1986); republished in *The Collected Stories* (Viking, 1992). Reproduced by permission of the author's estate.

11. Mary O'Donnell, 'The Black Church', from *Empire* (Arlen House, 2018). Reproduced by permission of the author and Arlen House.

12. Éilís Ní Dhuibhne, 'Miss Moffat Goes to Town'. An extended version of this story was published as 'Lemon Curd' in *Little Red and Other Stories* (Blackstaff Press, 2020). Reproduced by permission of the author and Blackstaff Press.

13. Mirsad Ibišević, 'Emigrant' (2022). Reproduced by permission of the author.

14. Caitlín Nic Íomhair, 'Cíocras'. Originally published in *Comhar* 80.4 (Aibreán 2020). Translated as 'Relentless' by the author (2022). Reproduced by permission of the author and *Comhar*.

15. Melatu Uche Okorie, 'Arrival' (2022). Reproduced by permission of the author.

16. Kevin Power, 'Catastrophe' (2022). Reproduced by permission of the author.

17. Caitriona Lally, 'Tramlines' (2022). Reproduced by permission of the author.

Every attempt has been made to contact copyright holders for permission to publish. Anyone wishing to assert their rights with regard to the contents of this anthology should contact OUP.

Acknowledgements

The editors wish to thank research assistant Orlaith Darling, and to acknowledge the help of the following: Ruth Archbold, John Brannigan, Bronagh Ćatibušić, Helen Constantine, Bernard O'Donoghue, Kelly Matthews, Helena Mulkerns, Máirín Nic Eoin, Michael Pierse, Elly Shaw, Frank Shovlin, and the library staff, Trinity College Dublin.